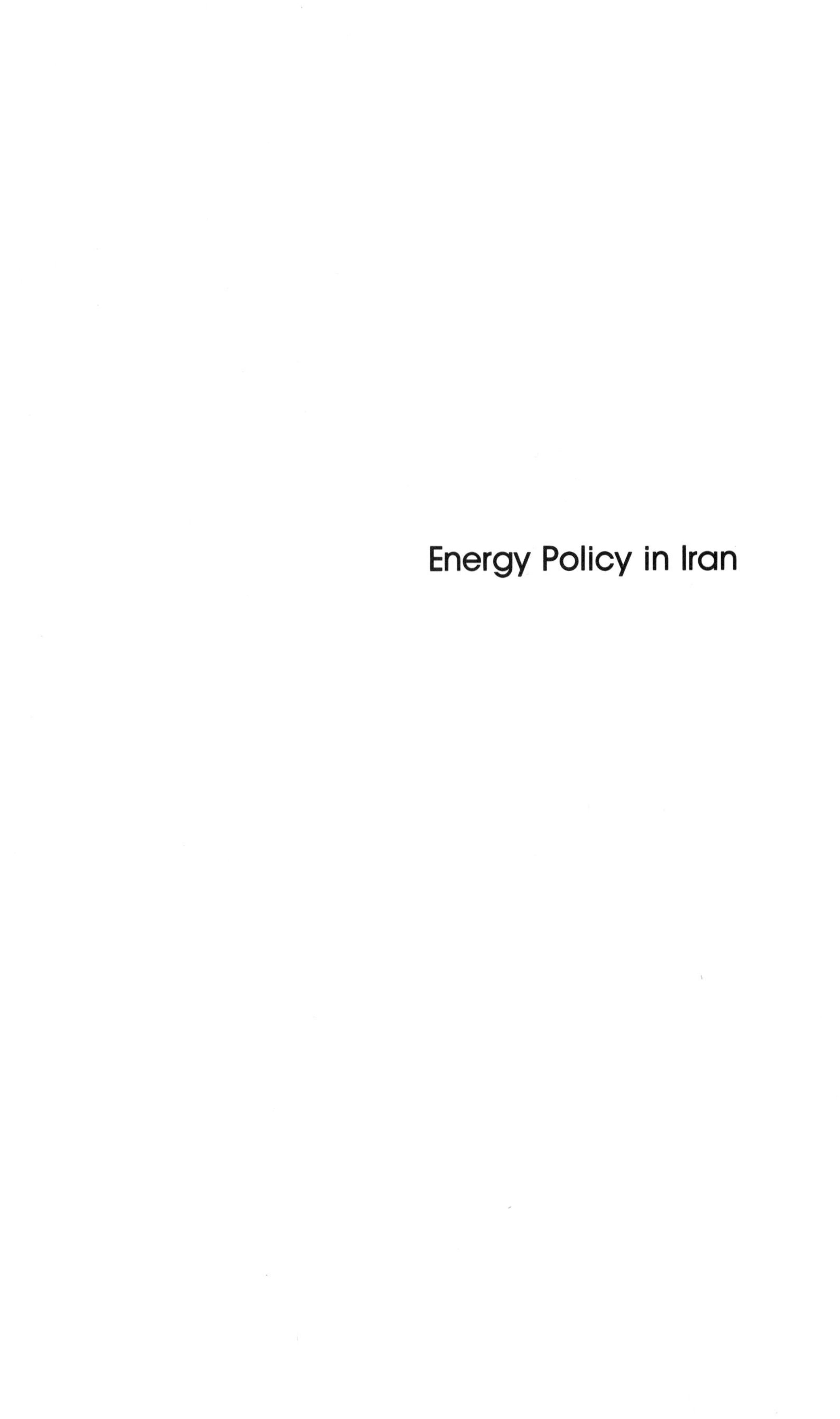

Energy Policy in Iran

ENERGY POLICY IN IRAN

Domestic Choices and International Implications

Bijan Mossavar-Rahmani

Pergamon Press

NEW YORK • OXFORD • TORONTO • SYDNEY • PARIS • FRANKFURT

Pergamon Press Offices:

U.S.A.	Pergamon Press Inc., Maxwell House, Fairview Park, Elmsford, New York 10523, U.S.A.
U.K.	Pergamon Press Ltd., Headington Hill Hall, Oxford OX3 0BW, England
CANADA	Pergamon Press Canada Ltd., Suite 104, 150 Consumers Road, Willowdale, Ontario M2J 1P9, Canada
AUSTRALIA	Pergamon Press (Aust.) Pty. Ltd., P.O. Box 544, Potts Point, NSW 2011, Australia
FRANCE	Pergamon Press SARL, 24 rue des Ecoles, 75240 Paris, Cedex 05, France
FEDERAL REPUBLIC OF GERMANY	Pergamon Press GmbH, Hammerweg 6 6242 Kronberg/Taunus, Federal Republic of Germany

Library of Congress Cataloging in Publication Data

Mossavar-Rahmani, Bijan.
Energy policy in Iran.

(Pergamon policy studies on energy)
Bibliography: p.
Includes index.
1. Energy policy--Iran. 2. Power resources--Iran.
I. Title. II. Series.
HD9502.I712M67 1981 333.79'0955 80-27995
ISBN 0-08-026293-7

Printed in the United States of America

To my family

Contents

Preface

In September 1978 I left Tehran to take up an appointment as a Visiting Research Fellow at the Rockefeller Foundation in New York, in large part to prepare a study of energy options and strategies in Iran. My own experiences in Iran had convinced me that the government's energy policies--or lack of them--would ultimately prove catastrophic in economic, infrastructural, and even political terms. The existing sad state of affairs was primarily a consequence of the mismanagement that pervaded nearly all levels of government activity in Iran in the 1970s. But the profligacy and lack of policy direction in the energy sector were further aggravated by an acute gap in information flow both within the numerous energy planning bodies and among the rival institutions. Thus, for example, officials of the energy ministry, even the minister himself, were not privy to cost estimates for nuclear reactors then under construction under the auspices of the country's atomic energy organization. Similarly, the minister in charge of OPEC affairs had to struggle hard to obtain estimates of the country's proven oil reserves from officials of the national oil company. So it was that a country that flared large volumes of its vast natural gas reserves had set off to build one of the world's largest and costliest nuclear power programs; indeed, Iran was rapidly negotiating to buy more reactors than it could hope to pay for, staff, or operate efficiently.

By documenting the various energy supply strategies and assessing their relative pros and cons in the context of a broad national energy plan, I hoped to contribute to an informed debate among Iranian energy analysts and planners about the country's energy future. But it was not long after this project had started that Iran was rocked by a far-reaching revolution; I returned to the country in early 1979 to find that whatever energy planning apparatus had existed was rapidly disappearing as many educated Iranians left for the West. As a consequence of bureaucratic paralysis, exodus of foreign contractors, and increasing difficulty in obtaining spare parts, the energy infrastructure itself was also hard-hit; literally so in 1980 as the Iran-Iraq war broke out.

Despite changing circumstances--and perhaps because of them--it was important to complete this project. Looking forward to a time when political, economic, and social factors are more stable, this book assesses energy demand patterns, evaluates major energy supply sources, and recommends policy guidelines intended to comprise an integrated national energy plan for Iran.

But this book has two other purposes as well. First, it is intended to provide some useful insights for other developing countries, particularly those facing similar energy options. Second, this book is to serve as a reminder that in addition to its strategic importance by sheer fact of geography, Iran remains a potential force in international energy markets despite its reduced role in the past three years.

I am grateful to many persons for assistance in the preparation of this study. Mason Willrich, former Director of International Relations at the Rockefeller Foundation first suggested that I come to New York to write this book. I am also indebted to his successor, Edwin A. Deagle, Jr. for continued encouragement and to other colleagues at the Rockefeller Foundation whose friendship and good humor proved invaluable during the course of this study. The generous support of the Rockefeller Foundation itself is of course gratefully acknowledged. Parts of this book developed out of a study prepared for the California Seminar on International Security and Foreign Policy and several lectures at Harvard University. The statistical material was collected over a several-year period in Iran with the help of numerous friends who also offered insights into the workings of the energy sector. Without them, this study would not have been possible.

Finally, I thank my wife Sharmin, herself an energy analyst, for her many helpful suggestions and above all, for her inspiration.

List of Tables

Table

Introduction

Wherever you dig in Iran, it has been said, if you don't strike oil, you will at least uncover ancient history. Sometimes you strike both in the same place.

So it was that the first discovery in 1908 of oil in commercial quantities in the Middle East was in the shadow of the Masjid-i-Suleiman fire temple, one of dozens of Zoroastrian fire temples scattered about Iran that used flared natural gas seepages in religious ceremonies.

The first recorded oil well was in ancient Iran and the first recorded oil tax was levied there. Over two thousand years ago, uses had been found for oil and a crude refining method was designed. Oil was drawn out of shallow wells and hauled away in goatskin bags, and the refining process yielded three products: salt, bitumen, and oil. The bitumen was used in binding bricks and other construction work, caulking ships, waterproofing pottery, and even as an adhesive for setting jewelry. The oil was used as fuel for lamps and for medicinal purposes; it was believed to be particularly effective in curing camels of mange. Armies used it in defense battlements, boiling it in cauldrons and pouring it on attacking troops, or using it for flaming arrow tips.

Thus oil, even then, was of value to virtually every segment of society although on a scale so comparatively small that today more oil is used in minutes than in the several preceding centuries. An important part of this oil, now as then, derives from Iran's vast reservoirs.

Before the Islamic revolution of 1978-79, Iran was producing an average of 5.5 million barrels per day (b/d) of oil, or over 10 percent of the world total, and exporting all but the 500,000 b/d that were consumed internally. Iran thus ranked as the world's fourth largest producer of oil (after the Soviet Union, the United States, and Saudi Arabia) and the second largest exporter after Saudi Arabia.

By mid-1981, however, Iran's oil output had dropped to an estimated 1.4 million b/d as a consequence of the continuing revolutionary turmoil and the border war with Iraq, and in all likelihood the country will be unwilling and perhaps unable in the near future to return to its previous production levels. At the same time, domestic consumption of oil products is expected to increase rapidly once the political situation stabilizes and the economy recovers, further reducing the availability of oil for export purposes. Indeed, by the 1990s Iran may export no more than a million barrels per day unless it can develop non-oil energy supplies, increase oil production from existing fields, and develop new ones. Yet the required massive investment and large number of foreign technicians may preclude the effort.

In examining Iran's domestic energy options and strategies and their international implications, this book begins by looking at how domestic energy strategies--in the oil, natural gas, and nuclear power sectors, for example--will affect not only Iran's own course of development but the world energy regime generally.

Then attention is drawn to Iran's domestic energy requirements. Historical patterns of demand by fuel and end-use are reviewed before turning to consider Iran's likely future needs vis-a-vis its anticipated economic growth.

While comprehensive information on the post-revolution performance of the economy generally, and on developments in the energy sector specifically, is not yet available, it is clear that the turmoil in Iran has led to a slowing down of economic growth beginning in the latter part of 1978 and continuing into 1981. Correspondingly, energy demand, which is very sensitive to economic growth, has not increased as rapidly as had been projected earlier, and new construction projects and facilities are behind schedule. Yet the thrust and direction of pre-revolution projections of energy demand --the only detailed ones currently available--remain more or less unchanged; one of the two projections of future energy demand used in this book is a revised version of an earlier forecast, modified to reflect, as well as possible under the circumstances, the changes that have taken place in Iran's energy sector during the last three years.

Part III describes Iran's energy resource base and the various fuel supply options. Oil, natural gas, hydropower, coal, solid and miscellaneous fuels, nuclear power and electricity are dealt with separately.

Part IV reviews the state of the Iranian petrochemical industry, once heralded as the vanguard of the industrialization effort, but now facing an uncertain future.

Finally, this book concludes with a set of components of a national energy plan for Iran. Most of these policy guidelines were proposed at one time or another before the revolution, but were not acted on by the former regime.

The first post-revolution government seemed at least to pay lip service to charting a new course for the country's energy future based on a more realistic and rational assessment of the national interest than was done in the past. Whether it will be possible to act with speed and deliberation in drawing up and implementing an integrated national energy plan under current political circumstances is highly doubtful. Yet in the aftermath of the revolution, it is perhaps more urgent than ever to estimate potential energy demand by region, fuel source, and end-use sector; to evaluate the availability and cost of alternative energy sources; and to examine the economic, political, technical, and social aspects of alternative programs for expanding energy use in Iran.

The size and scope of the energy infrastructure will be massive; indeed, Iran may face expenditures totaling over $50 billion by the turn of the century on power generating facilities, refineries, pipelines, dams, and the like, to meet even the most conservative projections of demand. Repairs to facilities damaged during the Iran-Iraq war will cost additional billions of dollars.

A delay in building up this infrastructure may damage more than just the economy. Any government in Tehran would do well to remember that public disillusionment with the Shah and his "great civilization" program was fueled in no small way by the persistent power brownouts and blackouts that plagued Iran throughout most of the 1970s.

Reliable economic data for Iran have always been difficult to collect; the problem is even more acute since the revolution. There has been a significant turnover in government officials, disrupting and at times paralyzing such bureaucratic operations as data collection, analysis, and long-range energy and economic planning.

In addition to the author's own files, this study has drawn heavily on three comprehensive reports dealing with Iran's energy position, these prepared either by or for the Iranian government. The first two studies are <u>A Long-Range Energy Plan for Iran</u>, prepared in 1977 by SRI International and Yekom Consultants (hereinafter referred to as the SRI study), and <u>Power Study of Iran 1974-1975</u>, prepared by the Montreal Engineering Co., Ltd., a Canadian consulting firm, in 1975 (Monenco study). The third is a series of unpublished internal reports by the Iranian government's principal national planning bureau, the Plan and Budget Organization (P&BO), only months before the revolution.[1]

NOTES

1. The P&BO's data on domestic energy requirements and supplies are based on the Iranian calendar only. These dates are converted to Gregorian calendar years by adding 621 years. Thus the Iranian calendar year 1356 becomes 1977 and so on, although in reality 1356 began on March 22, 1977 and ended on March 21, 1978.

I

General Framework

1 Iran in an International Setting

THE CHANGING STRUCTURE OF THE OIL MARKET

Projections of world demand in the 1980s for oil produced by members of the Organization of the Petroleum Exporting Countries (OPEC) have recently been downscaled to reflect expectations of slower economic growth and more efficient energy use in the industrial countries as a response to high prices.

Studies prepared in 1979-80, for example, project a mean estimate of 1985 world demand for OPEC oil of 34.3 million b/d as compared to a mean estimate of 41.0 million b/d for studies prepared as recently as 1977-78.[1]

Most analysts are doubtful, however, that the OPEC countries will be prepared to raise their total oil output to meet even these moderate estimates of world demand. Indeed, it now appears that the OPEC countries will produce no more than their combined 1979 level of 30.7 million b/d at least through the end of the present decade.

The latest study by the International Energy Agency, for example, estimates OPEC oil production in 1985 at 30.0 million b/d, down from an estimate of 37.5 million b/d published by the same Agency only two years earlier.[2]

Thus there is the expectation of a notional shortfall in worldwide availability of oil of about 4.0 million b/d in 1985, growing by another several million b/d by 1990.

Of course, there cannot be a gap between supply and demand in the real market; supply and demand will balance as adjustments are made through some combination of

- substantially higher real energy prices, resulting in higher rates of inflation as well as in lower rates of economic growth and its consequential implications for employment;

- stepped-up production of indigenous energy resources;
- greater efficiency in energy use.

While the latter two adjustments are more desirable, most analysts agree that it will be difficult to implement them in the short run. The industrial countries have pledged themselves yet again to set up a common strategy to reduce their consumption of imported oil and to accelerate the development of alternative sources of energy. Crash programs will be launched to develop synthetic fuels and solar power, the use of nuclear technology may be expanded, and additional conservation measures will be implemented.

But it should not be ignored that throughout the 1980s--and probably for much longer--the world economy will remain crucially dependent on oil and most of the free world will continue to depend on the OPEC countries, especially those in the Middle East, even if the rate of growth of that dependence slows or gradually is reversed. If demand for OPEC oil remains inelastic, it follows that the international oil market will be supply-constrained in the years ahead, much as it has been in the past decade. Moreover, political upheavals, terrorism, or accidents which create supply interruptions could have a more powerful effect in the future, and expectation of such possibilities may further add to upward pressure on prices.

A chronically tight and volatile oil market, if one does in fact persist, could strongly affect the world economy.[3] First, explosive price increases of the type experienced in 1979 could trigger a major recession which subsequently might produce at least a short-term slack oil market and falling real prices for OPEC oil. This could set the stage for another round of price explosions once recovery begins. In addition to the economic losses involved, such a vicious cycle could create monetary chaos worldwide, periodically creating huge surplus recycling burdens and making the planning and execution of national economic policies very difficult in both the oil-importing and exporting countries.

Second, unstable price behavior during the 1980s might add to the difficulty of making investment decisions on alternative energy resources, most of which now cost more than oil and require at least a decade to become operational. If the price of oil is allowed to rise at a steady rate, and is seen to approach or exceed the price of alternatives, then investments could become attractive. But much higher real oil prices entail further very large redistributions of wealth, and for many countries, severe economic, political and social costs.

Third, energy price swings might create especially troublesome problems for the poorer oil-importing countries. Rapid increases in oil prices drain scarce foreign exchange. Recession in the industrial countries leads to protectionism and reduced demand for raw materials and manufactured goods from the developing countries. Persistent balance-of-payments difficulties in the advanced countries could exhaust the availability of both commercial and concessionary lending for poorer developing countries, for whom sagging economic development and perhaps even insolvency might result.

Clearly, such a situation is undesirable insofar as the OPEC countries are concerned. Yet no early relief in the form of increased oil output can be expected from them as a group for the events leading to and following the revolution in Iran have forced OPEC to think again about matching oil output levels with the capacity of their economies to absorb oil revenues without serious political, economic, and social disruptions.[4]

Until recently, the decisions affecting the rate of oil production in the OPEC countries were generally made by the large international oil companies or majors, whose principal interest was to maximize short-term operating revenues by producing, refining and selling as much oil from each field and each country as the world market would absorb. Little or no consideration was given to the impact of such decisions on the amount of oil that could ultimately be recovered from these fields, the ability of the producing country's social, political and economic institutions to absorb their tremendous oil revenues, or the need to conserve part of the oil to help meet that country's own long-term requirements.

In the early 1970s, as a result of important structural changes in the world oil market, decisions affecting output began to be made by the oil-exporting governments themselves. However, as many of them faced low and still falling oil prices on the one hand, and ambitious development programs on the other, they scrambled to increase revenues through stepped-up oil production and exports, with little regard for the consequences.

This export and spending spree probably would have continued had it not been for the revolution in Iran. Its impact was twofold. First, the Shah's overblown modernization program--encouraged by zealous western salesmen--helped to hasten his downfall and demonstrated the danger of fast, unplanned spending. Second, the Iranian oil workers' strikes that helped oust the Shah also precipitated a crisis atmosphere in which a major oil price shock was inevitable. The ensuing price and revenue increases allowed the oil exporters to plan production cutbacks in the interest of better resource management without compromising their spending programs.

The wasteful and eventually disastrous Iranian experience prompted the other OPEC countries to redefine and reassess their own capacity to absorb revenues without overheating their economies and rocking the social and political order.

In many of these countries, inflationary spending programs caused severe and visible maldistribution of wealth; raised expectations that could not be quickly fulfilled; de-stabilized demographic and regional balances; and created urban congestion with all of the attendant problems. In the Moslem countries, westernization clashed with Islamic fundamentalism. Some felt a growing threat from the many foreign workers, needed for massive construction programs, who were demanding not only treatment and benefits that then accrued only to the nationals of these countries, but even, eventually, political participation in host country affairs.

Yet even as the OPEC countries become more conscious of the limitations on their spending, they have still to develop a practical definition of absorptive capacity as a measure of orderly growth.

In the 1970s, government officials in these countries appeared guided by the principle that their economies could absorb limitless imports of capital, intermediate and consumption goods and services. For some, certainly military spending was a bottomless pit. Funds not spent on the military, others reasoned, could be invested abroad, primarily in the form of liquid assets.

These attitudes are beginning to change and a consensus seems to be emerging that absorptive capacity should be measured in terms of the amount of revenue that can be spent in each country without waste and de-stabilization.

More attention is paid to the real returns on foreign investments. At present, the OPEC countries have little financial incentive to retain high oil export levels and to invest surplus revenues abroad since investments, most notably in the United States, often have been disappointing because of the effects of inflation and exchange rate fluctuations. This problem has been somewhat compounded by uncertainties over the security of investments after the U.S. freeze of Iranian assets two years ago.

The change in OPEC oil policies is also prompted by a heightened conservationist concern vis-a-vis oil production. As the OPEC countries re-examined the financial trade-offs between keeping their oil in the ground, or producing it to invest either in domestic economic development or foreign assets, or both, they are also assessing optimum rates of production from longer-term economic and technical perspectives. They are becoming aware that as a result of too rapid a rate of production, their single most important source of foreign exchange earnings may run out before they have had a chance to build up sustainable, non-oil, and preferably industrialized economies, with enough oil left over to meet domestic needs until alternative sources of energy become available.

Some key countries have adopted or are now adopting go-slow production policies--a decision to produce at below their technically feasible capacity levels; moreover, at least one country, Saudi Arabia, is reported to be postponing capital investments to increase its capacity.

Thus it is increasingly important to distinguish between the two determinants of OPEC oil availability: technical and policy-induced capacity.

On the technical side, each OPEC country has an installed oil production capacity (determined not only by output from the oil wells themselves but by processing, transportation, interim storage, and terminal facilities as well) and a sustainable capacity (maximum level of total system production that can be sustained for a period of several months). Both installed and sustainable capacities are fixed over the short run. In 1981, OPEC's combined installed capacity stood at an estimated 41.1 million b/d; total sustainable capacity stood at 33.5 million b/d. However, it is now widely recognized that not every OPEC country is willing to meet demand for its oil by producing at or even near sustainable levels; policy considerations have already lowered the available capacity (allowables) in several key OPEC countries including Saudi Arabia, Iran, Kuwait, and the United Arab Emirates. Such policy-induced constraints on production result from a concern over economic, political, and social de-stabilization in some countries resulting from too rapid a rate of spending; too rapid a rate of depletion of oil resources; disappointing returns on foreign investments of surplus oil revenues; and growing internal pressures to reassess oil policies.

Table 1.1 details installed, sustainable, and available capacities of the OPEC countries in 1981. It should be noted that the aggregate figures here represent not concerted OPEC-wide proration but a combination of unilateral production decisions by individual countries. Indeed, OPEC has so far been unable to prorate production among its members, although several formulae based on such factors as volume of proven reserves, depletion rates, population, per capita income, and historical production patterns have been considered from time to time. Failure to adopt and implement a formal production program has stemmed from reluctance on the part of member countries to abdicate their right to unilateral decisions on matters they consider sovereign; difficulties in reaching consensus over a formula agreeable to all at once; and the problems of enforcing the allocations. OPEC has therefore never been, and probably never will become, a cartel in the traditional sense; rather it can best be described as a price-setting association.

Table 1.1. OPEC Crude Oil Production Capacity in 1981

(million b/d)

	Installed Capacity[a]	Sustainable Capacity[b]	Available Capacity[c]	Production in 1st Half 1981[d]
Algeria	1.2	1.2	1.2	0.9
Ecuador	0.3	0.2	0.2	0.2
Gabon	0.3	0.2	0.2	0.2
Indonesia	1.8	1.6	1.6	1.6
Iran	6.5	4.0	4.0	1.4
Iraq	4.0	3.5	3.5	0.9
Kuwait	2.9	2.5	1.3	1.2
Libya	2.5	2.1	2.1	1.6
Neutral Zone[e]	0.7	0.6	0.6	0.5
Nigeria	2.5	2.2	2.2	1.9
Qatar	0.7	0.6	0.6	0.5
Saudi Arabia	12.5	10.0	10.0	10.0
United Arab Emirates	2.6	2.4	1.6	1.6
Venezuela	2.6	2.4	2.2	2.2
Total	41.1	33.5	31.3	24.7

[a]Installed capacity includes all aspects of crude oil production, including not only actual production but processing, transportation, interim storage, and loading terminal capacities as well.

[b]Sustainable capacity denotes the maximum level of production, again of the total system, that can be sustained for at least several months.

[c]Available capacity is the production ceiling set by a producing country and reflects technical, economic or political considerations; these ceilings are usually set for an annual average output and may be exceeded in any given month.

[d]Projected.

[e]Neutral Zone production is jointly shared by Saudi Arabia and Kuwait.

Source: Author's estimates based on trade sources.

Some OPEC countries are also restricting output to slow down or reverse the decline in their proven reserves-to-production ratios. In 1980, OPEC's aggregate proven reserves of oil stood at 450 billion barrels. At a production rate of about 30 million b/d, reserves will last only 40 years for the group as a whole--probably much less for countries with high production rates and small proven reserves. In 1960 OPEC's proven reserves-to-production ratio was nearly 70:1; in 1970 it was 50:1, reflecting annual production in OPEC countries far in excess of additions to proven reserves. Between 1971 and 1980, for example, total OPEC production stood at about 80 billion barrels, whereas, net additions to reserves totaled less than 30 billion barrels.

Significantly, exploratory and development drilling in the OPEC countries has been meager compared with other oil-producing countries. For example, in 1978 less than 1,800 wells were drilled in the OPEC countries out of a world total of nearly 61,000--only three percent. Of these wells, only 371 were wildcats, out of a world total of 15,258, of which 10,677 were drilled in the United States alone; this, despite the fact that half of the world's proven reserves of oil have been discovered in the OPEC countries, and these countries present perhaps the most promising potential for future finds.[5]

Several countries adopted a policy of carrot-and-stick in 1979 to induce their former concessionaires and others with the technical know-how, managerial skills and venture capital to step up exploration and development activities in return for offtake entitlements for whatever oil is discovered. In 1979, Libya and Algeria, for example, required a commitment to explore for oil as a precondition for continued access to existing production. With a general softening of the world oil market since 1980, however, these requirements, for the most part, have been shelved, although they are likely to be reintroduced once the market tightens again. But even if these efforts engage the companies with resources and skills in exploration and improved recovery techniques, and even if such efforts are successful, the net effect over the medium- to long-term may only be to prevent further erosion in combined OPEC output.

But perhaps more important than the question of how much oil the individual OPEC countries will be technically able and politically prepared to produce in the coming decades is one that tends to be ignored: given the restrictions--some self-imposed, others not--on oil production, on the one hand, and growing internal requirements for oil products on the other, how much oil will OPEC actually have for export?

Many analyses of the world oil market have used OPEC oil production data and OPEC oil export data interchangeably, largely because domestic consumption of oil products in these countries was small, both in absolute terms and relative to the size of their combined output.[6] But that picture is changing and it is important to make the distinction between the two, given the rise in OPEC oil consumption at home.

Iran's Significant Role

In making that distinction, this study focuses on one country --Iran--whose oil consumption historically has been by far the highest among the OPEC countries.[7] Moreover, Iran is important to the world oil market for at least two other reasons. First, despite dramatic output cutbacks since 1978, Iran remains a potentially significant producer and exporter of oil, particularly at the margin. Table 1.2 gives detailed statistics on Iran's oil reserves, production, and exports between 1974 and 1980. Second, decisions made in Iran regarding the development of its oil production capacity and its overall internal energy supply strategies will be watched very closely by other oil producers, and the impact of Iran's choices will, in all likelihood, be felt beyond that country's borders.

Iran is rich in oil resources; its proven reserves have been estimated at just under 60 billion barrels but the actual figure is probably much higher. The Shah's government long pursued a policy based on maximizing oil output and sales to increase oil production by at least 1.5 to 2.0 million b/d, almost to the 7.5 million b/d level. While that target was unrealistic in view of the physical limitations of the reservoirs, output would probably have remained between 5.5 and 6.0 million b/d through the 1980s, had not the Shah been overthrown.

Even at those levels, the impact of a growing consumption of oil products within Iran would soon make itself felt. Iran's population, currently about 37 million, is expected to grow to 55 million by the turn of the century. Internal sales of oil products were about 500,000 b/d in 1980; this level would have been 200,000 to 300,000 b/d higher if industrial and economic activity had not been disrupted by the revolution. Curtailing the size of the Iranian military has also contributed to the drops in consumption.

These losses will be recovered quickly once political and economic stability return, however. Earlier government plans called for slowing down the increase in domestic oil consumption from the average of 15 to 20 percent prevalent in the 1970s, to just under 10 percent; according to these projections, total domestic consumption would approach 1.0 million b/d by 1982, 1.5 million b/d by 1987, and 3.0 million b/d by the year 2000.

Table 1.2. Iran's Crude Oil in an International Setting

	1974	1975	1976	1977	1978	1979	1980
Reserves[a] (billion barrels)	60.0	66.0	64.5	63.0	62.0	59.0	58.0
percentage of OPEC	14.2	13.6	14.3	14.4	14.1	13.3	13.3
percentage of world	9.6	9.2	9.8	9.9	9.6	9.2	9.0
Production (thousand b/d)	6,022	5,350	5,883	5,663	5,242	3,168	1,622
percentage of OPEC	19.6	19.7	19.1	18.1	17.6	10.2	6.0
percentage of world	10.7	10.0	10.2	9.5	8.7	5.0	2.7
Exports (thousand b/d)[b]	5,369	4,671	5,214	4,867	4,447	2,407	n.a.
percentage of OPEC	19.7	19.4	19.0	17.6	17.0	9.0	n.a.
percentage of world	17.1	16.4	16.3	15.1	14.2	7.5	n.a.

[a]Proven reserves as of January 1.

[b]In addition to crude oil, Iran historically has exported significant quantities of refined oil products; such exports totaled 147,000 b/d in 1973, 163,000 b/d in 1974, 215,000 b/d in 1975, 116,000 b/d in 1976, 119,000 b/d in 1977, 128,000 b/d in 1978, and 173,000 b/d in 1979.

Source: Organization of the Petroleum Exporting Countries, Annual Statistical Bulletin 1979, OPEC, Vienna, 1980.

As will be discussed later, these projections were based on the assumption of economic growth averaging about 9 percent per year over the next twenty years--which is unlikely to be achieved. Even if it were able to do so, the new Iranian government will probably not pursue the rapid economic development and industrialization necessary to sustain such a growth rate. Moreover, Iran is part of a world economy in which projections of long-term economic growth for the industrial countries have dropped from an average annual rate of 4.0-4.5 percent to 2.5-3.0 percent or less, resulting in expectations of lower economic growth in the developing countries as well--in Iran, perhaps, to 5.0-7.0 percent a year.

On the other hand, if Iran does not develop alternative domestic energy sources such as natural gas soon enough, or if it increases the distribution of oil products in its underdeveloped rural and provincial areas, domestic oil demand may indeed grow at the rates projected earlier.

It should also be noted that a rapid rise in demand for oil products and the extensive damage to the country's largest oil refinery at Abadan resulting from the war with Iraq will require construction of a large refinery every second or third year beginning in the early 1980s. Ironically enough, even with these refineries, the gap between Iran's supply of and demand for certain products, and specifically the disproportionate demand for middle-distillates, will make it necessary to continue importing these products into a country that sits on one of the world's largest reserves of oil. This middle-distillate gap has embarrassed Iran more than once, most recently when it was reported in mid-1979 that Iran's post-revolutionary government was negotiating to import kerosene from the United States.

Iran exported over 95 percent of its oil in the early 1970s. By the 1990s, it may be exporting no more than a few hundred thousand barrels per day unless it can develop non-oil energy supplies and/or increase oil production capacity substantially through enhanced recovery from existing fields and the discovery of new ones. Yet these efforts may not be forthcoming because massive investments and the need for large numbers of foreign technicians may prevent them. Furthermore, Iran may not even feel a pressing need to make these efforts, at least in the 1980s, if the real price of oil continues to climb, compensating for revenue losses that result from low exports.

Indeed, Iran's experience may become the rule in the years ahead. Given the limited incentive for many OPEC countries to export additional oil, on the one hand, and increasing world demand for oil, on the other, pressure will continue to build for higher prices. Higher prices and higher revenues will reduce even further the incentive to export, resulting in a vicious oil price cycle.

In table 1.3 a reasonable range of Iranian oil production levels is projected against a range of domestic consumption levels for the period 1980-2000. Even in high production-low consumption conditions, Iran will be unable during the next two decades to regain its former position as a leading exporter of oil in the world market. In a low production-high consumption situation, Iran will be exporting only small quantities of oil by the year 2000, if any; the inevitable problems for Iran, as well as for the world's oil importers, need not be elaborated upon.

Table 1.3. Projected Oil Production, Exports, and Revenues in Iran: 1980-2000

(million b/d)

	1980[a]	1985	2000
Production	1.6	3.0-4.0	3.0-4.5
Consumption[b]	0.5	0.7-1.0	1.3-2.0
Exports	1.1	2.0-3.3	1.0-3.2
Revenues (billions of current U.S. dollars)[c]	13	37-60	73-234

[a]Based on preliminary estimates.

[b]See Chapter 4 for detailed projections of domestic oil and energy consumption.

[c]Based on a 10 percent average annual increase in the nominal price of oil (1985 = $50 a barrel; 2000 = $200 a barrel).

Source: Author's estimates.

OTHER ENERGY DECISIONS IN IRAN--INTERNATIONAL IMPLICATIONS

Decisions involving Iran's internal energy policies in three other areas will also have important implications for the international community.

Natural Gas

Iran's future conduct with regard to the development of its natural gas resources is potentially very significant since its vast resources could make it one of the world's major exporters of this source of clean, safe, and versatile energy (see table 1.4).

World natural gas consumption has been rising steadily over the past decade, with 1979 consumption rates about 50 percent higher than 1969 rates. At 51 trillion cubic feet (tcf), world natural gas consumption in 1979 was 19 percent of world primary energy consumption, although the rates varied considerably from country to country, with a high of 45 percent in the Netherlands, 26 percent in the United States, and only about 6 percent in Japan.

Natural gas consumption in the industrial countries is expected to rise over the next twenty years in both absolute and relative terms; 1985 demand is estimated at about 32 tcf, rising to 35 tcf by the year 2000. Given total projected natural gas production within the industrial countries themselves of about 25 tcf in 1985, falling off to 17 tcf in 2000, import requirements are expected to total at least 7 tcf in 1985 and 16 tcf in 2000.

These projections assume that coal or nuclear energy or both will be major substitutes for oil. Two factors, however, limit the extent of such substitution: the reduced availability of these alternative fuels because of physical, political, economic, and environmental constraints; and restricted inter-fuel substitution in the short- to medium-term because of technological and infrastructural limitations.

With declining domestic natural gas output in the industrial countries and the expected shortfalls in oil and such alternatives as coal and nuclear power, the natural gas import requirements of the industrial countries may well climb sharply beginning in the latter half of the 1980s.

Most of those requirements can be met from the Middle East and North Africa, particularly from Iran and Algeria. Other important sources would be Indonesia, an OPEC member, and such non-OPEC countries as the Soviet Union, Mexico, Brunei, and Malaysia.

Until recently, high transportation costs and high investment requirements placed natural gas at a competitive

words in which certain assumptions have been made and something other than the assumptions necessarily follows in virtue of those assumptions" (24b18). A syllogism involves three terms, which Aristotle calls the extremes and the middle. These are grouped in two premisses, each a proposition connecting one of the extremes with the middle term. From this it is possible to deduce a valid conclusion connecting the extremes. Thus

Mortality is predicated of all human beings
Humanity is predicated of all Athenians
Therefore Mortality must necessarily be predicated of all Athenians.

(This was the form in which Aristotle set it out. We are more used to

All men are mortal
All Athenians are men
Therefore all Athenians are mortal)

Aristotle's genius lay, first, in using letters to represent the terms, algebraically, as we might say, so that the logic becomes clear regardless of the actual statements (which may arouse illogical emotional responses), and, second, in seeing the patterns into which the syllogism may fall. He recognized three "figures." In the first

A
is predicated of B (middle term)
which is predicated of C

(Aristotle uses alpha, beta, gamma, of course.) In the second

M (middle term)
is predicated of N ("nearer")
and also of O

(Aristotle uses MNX, which were consecutive in the Greek alphabet.) In the third

P ("further")
and R
are both predicated of S [5]

This way of setting things out explains Aristotle's use of the words "nearer to" and "further from" the middle. It also explains why he saw the fourth figure of medieval logic only as a mood of the first: his figures are based on the position of the middle term. "Without a middle term a syllogism does not take place" (66a28; cf. 40b37 ff.). Each figure has a certain number of "moods." Thus in the first figure the first proposition or major premiss is always universal, but may be positive or negative. The minor premiss may be universal or particular so that by combining these, four moods are possible.

It will be convenient, provided that we recognize that it is implicit, not explicit, in Aristotle, to present the syllogism as it was set out in the logical system which derived from him. The conclusion will contain a subject (S) and predicate (P); the middle term is called M, and the same letters are used in all the figures. The first figure is set out:

$$\begin{array}{cc} M & P \\ S & M \\ \hline S & P \end{array}$$

The second figure:

$$\begin{array}{cc} P & M \\ S & M \\ \hline S & P \end{array}$$

The third figure:

$$\begin{array}{cc} M & P \\ M & S \\ \hline S & P \end{array}$$

The Scholastics acknowledged a fourth figure (which was discovered by the great doctor Galen)

$$\begin{array}{cc} P & M \\ M & S \\ \hline S & P \end{array}$$

In the thirteenth century Peter the Spaniard devised a barbarous mnemonic in doggerel Latin displaying all the moods:

> BARBARA CELARENT DARII FERIOque prioris:
> CESARE CAMESTRES FESTINO BAROCO secundae:
> tertia DARAPTI DISAMIS DATISI FELAPTON
> BOCARDO FERISON habet: quarta insuper addit
> BRAMANTIP CAMENES DIMARIS FESAPO FRESISON

The vowels of the capitalized words represent AEIO propositions and show the valid conclusions in the only valid patterns. (The consonants MSPC immediately after a vowel, and not others, are significant. M (muta) = transpose premisses; S (simpliciter) = simple conversion; P (per accidens) = convert by limitation; C (conversio) = substitute contradictory of conclusion for premiss. These convey the instructions for reducing the syllogism to what Aristotle thought a more cogent form.) Thus

All men are mortal	M a P
All Athenians are men	S a M

This is an example of the first figure; the mood is Barbara; a–a gives a for its conclusion. So

S a P	All Athenians are mortal

or again

Everything which lives moves	P a M
No stone moves	S e M

This is an example of the second figure; the mood is Camestres; a–e gives e for its conclusion. So

S e P	No stone lives

Here is a different example

Some clergymen are dishonest	M i P
Rev. John Jones is a clergyman	S a M

This is an example of the first figure. But there is no mood of the first figure beginning i–a–. It follows that no valid conclusion can be drawn. It will be noticed that a universal affirmative conclusion results from the first figure only; it is, says Aristotle, the hardest to establish and the easiest to overthrow (42b33). It will be noticed also that the second figure gives only negative conclusions (38a8), and the third only particular conclusions (29a16). Furthermore, for any syllogism to be valid, at least one premiss must be affirmative, at least one premiss must be universal, and at least one premiss must be similar to the conclusion, that is assertorial, apodeictic, or problematic (41b6).

Now Aristotle speaks at one point of hypothetical proof (41a21). He means by this that one of the premisses may be a hypothesis or assumption ("let it be granted that . . .") rather than an accepted fact. This is important in two ways. Negatively, it was freely used in geometry. To take Aristotle's example, the diagonal of a square is either commensurable or incommensurable with the sides. If we start from the hypothesis of its commensurability, we reach the conclusion that odd numbers are equal to even. This is therefore a false hypothesis since it leads to a false conclusion. Therefore the diagonal is incommensurable with the sides. But the hypothesis also had its place in general argument. We may ask, for example, "Do you agree that in a democracy all citizens should have equal opportunities?" If our interlocutor concedes this, we have a basis from which to make valid hypothetical deductions; that is to say, that they follow validly from the hypothesis.

This is indeed important for our total understanding of the syllogism. It has sometimes been argued that the syllogism can give no new knowledge. One of the premisses must be universal, and that will already contain the conclusion. We cannot know that all men are mortal unless we already know that all Athenians are mortal. But this is not quite true. Aristotle has an important section on induction (68a15), which he treats syllogistically. His instance is as follows: Let A = long-lived, B = bileless, C = long-lived animals (man, horse, mule). The formal syllogism runs

All these animals are long-lived	C a A
All these animals are bileless	C a B

This is a third figure syllogism in Darapti, and the conclusion is

B i A Some bileless creatures are long-lived

But if, and only if, we can convert the second proposition not to a particular affirmative but to a universal affirmative, that is, if our list exhausts the catalog of bileless creatures, we should have

All these animals are long-lived	C a A
All bileless animals are these	B a C

This is now a first figure syllogism in Barbara, and the conclusion is

B a A All bileless animals are long-lived

It is doubtful whether this is the most fruitful approach to induction, but it is Aristotle's. However, it is a fact that we arrive at propositions inductively, not by enumerating all instances, but by generalizing from a large number. This is the method of procedure in science; it was Francis Bacon's formula for the scientific revolution. We observe a large number of particular instances, our mind leaps to a pattern, we lay down a generalization, and proceed to test it, and if all the instances confirm the generalization and none runs counter to it, our generalization, arrived at inductively, takes on the status of "a scientific law." It should be realized that such "laws" are never in fact more than hypothetical and are always liable to be refuted by fresh observations. Aristotle indeed knew this, and when he was not so preoccupied with the perfection of the syllogism in *Posterior Analytics* said something very similar: induction is a lucky shot at the middle term; one of his examples is to see someone talking to a millionaire and conclude that he is trying to borrow money (89a10). When the major premiss is reached by induction we may accept the general proposition without having proved it true for every part: we do not in fact examine all Athenians before inducing the proposition that all men are mortal. So that the syllogistic conclusion does give us knowledge, which we did not have before or had potentially rather than actually, though the knowledge is always in fact hypothetical. The syllogism, as Strawson[6] puts it, shows whether our statements square with one another, not whether they square with the facts. Still more clearly we acquire new knowledge when we accept the major premiss on the basis of authority. It is thus of paramount importance in deductive reasoning to examine the nature of our premisses. Proverbial saws, for example, make dangerous major premisses: many hands make light work, but too many cooks spoil the broth. And many arguments have fallen apart because the disputants, as Mark Pattison said of the cleaning-women shouting at one another from opposite doorways, have been arguing from different premisses.

IV *Demonstration as Knowledge*

Posterior Analytics passes from the general principles of reasoning to the particular example that Aristotle calls demonstration. Demonstration is a syllogism, which produces knowledge. Knowledge, without qualification, demands conviction that the cause from which the fact arises is the cause of that fact and that the fact cannot be otherwise (71b9). In syllogistic terms this demands not merely a valid syllogism but premisses, which are "true, primary, immediate, better known than, prior to and causative of the conclusion" (71b20). Aristotle makes an important distinction: the universal (which Plato gave metaphysical existence as Form) is in an absolute sense prior and more knowable, but to us the particular is prior in experience and more closely knowable; this was the basis of Ibn Roshd's (Averroës's) brilliant reconciliation of Plato, Aristotle, and Islam. Immediate premisses are of two kinds (72a7). One is the *axiom,* the self-evident truth, which is the precondition of any other learning. The other Aristotle called *thesis* and subdivides into *definition* and *hypothesis.* Euclidean geometry is a good example of a logical system of thought built up from a small number of axioms or common notions, definitions, and hypotheses or postulates. The full systematizing of geometry lay in the next generation, but Euclid did not leap like Athene fully armed from Zeus's head, and it will be scientific geometry that Aristotle has especially in mind; the illustrations which he uses are predominantly mathematical, and this fact has been used as evidence that *Posterior Analytics* is an early work,[7] written "under the tail of Plato," but the argument is not cogent, since mathematics provided the only obvious illustration. Aristotle's use of mathematics is important; for all his empiricism he is preoccupied with the search for necessary conclusions. The ultimate principles are not demonstrable; the attempt to demonstrate them leads us into either an infinite regress or a circular argument. Aristotle returns to this at the very end of *Posterior Analytics* (99b15 ff.). But the fact that none of the first principles is demonstrable leads us to ask whether the distinction between axioms and hypotheses is legitimate.

Scientific knowledge is concerned with facts that are necessarily true, and it must proceed from premisses that are necessarily true (73a20). More, scientific knowledge requires a universal relation between subject and predicate. First, the predicate must be true of every instance of the subject, without exception. Second, it must belong to the subject essentially, not accidentally. Third, it must be true of the subject in its own right, not as pertaining to some higher classification. The proposition "The angles of a triangle are equal to two right angles" is an example of scientific knowledge in Aristotle's sense, but "The angles of a geometrical figure are equal to two right angles" would offend against the first criterion, and "The angles of an isosceles triangle are equal to two right angles" against the third. It follows also that the fact of one science cannot be proved by the principles appropriate to another; we would be in trouble (to modernize his example) if we tried to handle Riemannian geometry by Euclidean techniques.

The remainder of the first book seems less fundamental. Aristotle discusses various forms of faulty reasoning and later contrasts scientific knowledge with sense perception (which deals in particulars) and opinion (which deals with the contingent where knowledge is concerned with the necessarily true). A long exposition argues against the possibility of an infinite chain of predication; that is to say, that appropriate first principles in each science are reached without an infinite regress, and, further, there is a finite number of steps from the most universal to the most particular. Much of the argument is frankly tedious, but Aristotle is too good a teacher not to include occasional "nuggets." Such are his allusion to Anacharsis's epigram that there are no flute-players in Russia because there are no vines (78b30: the flute is a wind instrument; to use the lungs makes you thirsty; to quench thirst you need wine; for wine you need grapes; for grapes you need vines), or his description of Plato's Theory of Forms as "twittering" (83a33). For the rest we may note his urgent arguments that universal demonstration is superior to particular, that affirmative demonstration is superior to negative, and that ostensive demonstration is superior to *reductio ad impossibile* (85a13 ff), and more particularly his continual insistence on the importance of the middle term for valid reasoning. And when he asserts (against Plato's Forms) that the fact that a term has a single meaning does not necessitate that it refers to a single entity (85b19), we might almost be reading Wittgenstein.

To the importance of the middle term he returns at the beginning of the second book. Turning to the topic of definition, he isolates four questions which we ask: Is S P? Why is S P? Does S exist? What is S? Aristotle gives examples: Is the sun in eclipse? Why is the sun in eclipse? Does a centaur exist? What is man? He suggests that all these questions are a search for a middle term. This is decidedly odd, for formally only the second question contains two elements and the search for a "middle term" to connect them, and this is not a syllogistic middle term, though Aristotle tries at one point to make it so (93a29). There is in fact some confusion. In a teleological system a question about existence implies a question about cause, and Aristotle seems to be using the phrase "middle term" loosely in this sense. But Aristotle is not thinking of substances so much as of attributes; he has really in mind that the definition of an attribute implies a relation to a subject and a cause for that relation. All the questions "Is there such a thing as an eclipse?" "What is an eclipse?" "Is the sun in eclipse?" demand an answer to the question "Why is the sun in eclipse?" Aristotle goes on to treat the relation between definition and demonstration. Definition and demonstration are distinct operations (91a7), and a definition cannot be demonstrated syllogistically, but we can use demonstration to arrive at a definition. For example, if A stands for eclipse, C for moon, and B for obstruction by the earth, we can construct a kind of syllogism whereby

eclipse (A)
is predicated of whatever has an obstruction between it and the
sun (B)
which is predicated of the moon (C),

a first figure syllogism in Barbara. We can take from this a definition of eclipse as an attribute of the moon: "loss of light due to the obstruction of the earth." But some definitions cannot be framed in the light of "middle terms"; the unit in arithmetic, for example, is a first principle. There are thus three types of definition: (a) an explanation of the meaning of a name without reference to the existence of the thing referred to; (b) definition which explains why a thing exists and is associated with demonstration; and (c) indemonstrable assumption of first principles (93b29). As Ross says, these correspond to Mill's derivative laws, empirical laws, and laws of nature.[8]

There follows a section of considerable difficulty. In *Physics*, as we shall see, Aristotle isolates four causes: formal, material, efficient, final. Here too (94a20) he isolates four causes: essence, necessitating ground, origin of motion, final. Three correspond; the fourth apparently does not. In his other treatment he argues that the three sometimes coalesce, and it looks as if here he is seeing yet another aspect of this group of causes. If so the passage may be early. But the argument is by no means clear. Nor is Aristotle much clearer when he considers the causal link between events which are separate in time; the earlier event can be inferred from the later but not the later from the earlier; there is here a problem over discontinuity. Aristotle could do with a dose of Bergson here. He has used his intellect to cut up the flow of reality into cinematographic stills called events, but reality is not like that.

He then returns to definition, and his Platonic schooling comes out. Plato had explained his science of dialectic in terms of collection and division. Plato's method of definition was to gather together under one head the several examples of the thing to be defined, and to subdivide until a definition applicable to that thing alone is found.[9] Thus in *The Sophist* angling is classified as a skill, acquisitive rather than productive, using force rather than persuasion, hunting rather than fighting, with a sentient not an inanimate object, seeking water animals not land animals, swimmers not flyers, using a blow not a net, by day not night, striking from below not above. Aristotle uses collection and division but uses them differently. He collects the attributes, which universally apply to the thing to be defined but to other things as well. Thus 3 has as attributes: it is a number, it is odd, it is prime, and it cannot be formed as the sum of two numbers (the unit did not count as a number); it shares the second quality with 5, the last two with 2, but the combination applies uniquely to 3. Division has its place in the correct analysis of these attributes. In general it is important to select only those attributes which pertain to the essence; to arrange them in logical order; and to ensure that the list is complete (97a23).

Then after a discussion of causality (in which his examples extend beyond mathematics to meteorology, zoology, and botany) Aristotle reaches his climax; he has, as Tredennick says, "repeatedly—by a dramatic instinct—whetted our appetite"[10] for it. What is the faculty by which we apprehend first principles? He postpones his answer to the very end. All animals have sense perception; in some the perception is held in memory; in rational beings collected memories give rise to "experience," that is the identification of the universal, the One corresponding to the memory, the power of generalizing. This is the starting point of all science and scholarship. So it is by induction that we reach knowledge of first principles, and the organ we use is intuitive reason (*nous*).

It cannot truthfully be said that *Posterior Analytics* is one of Aristotle's best works: Miss Anscombe called the first book his worst.[11] The main fault lies in straining the categorical syllogism beyond the weight it can possibly bear; Aristotle is entranced with his discovery and wants to use it as a key to unlock all doors. In addition, there are too many inconsistencies and obscurities. At the same time we must see it in context; it will not do to evaluate it as if it were a work by Toulmin and Strawson, or even Mill. It is a pioneering work, the first serious attempt to give a logical account of scientific reason. And whatever the defects of the whole, the last chapter, displaying the unbroken chain from sense perception to intuitive reason, is in its own way magnificent.

V "Topics"

Topics[12] is by comparison a minor work; it was, however, through Cicero's *Topics*, of some literary influence, touching Boethius, Erasmus, Bacon, and Milton, among others, and helping to mold the pattern of Elizabethan education. It is generally agreed that it was not all composed at the same time, books II-VI and the first part of book VII being written early, and book VIII appreciably later; there is controversy about book I and the remainder of book VII. "Topics" are (almost literally) commonplaces; they are, in Ross's words, "the pigeon-holes from which dialectic reasoning is to draw its arguments." Hence the gibe of one of Jonson's characters: "There's Aristotle, a meer commonplace fellow." [13] The purpose of the work is stated in the opening sentence: it is "to find a method by which we shall be able to reason about any proposed problem from generally accepted opinions and personally sustain an argument without self-contradiction" (100a18). Such reasoning Aristotle calls dialectical rather than demonstrative; it does not proceed from premisses which are certain truths. The language is a hit at Plato, who valued dialectic as highly as Aristotle valued his syllogism; still, Aristotle accords dialectical reasoning a status above eristic, or contentious reasoning (which Plato likewise scorns, calling it antilogic), let alone false reasoning. But though dialectical reasoning is not primary it has its place: first, as mental training, second, for conversation with non-philosophers on their own grounds, third, as a subsidiary means of clarification in philosophic knowledge.

A basic discussion of four different types of predicate follows. A predicate is a *definition* if it is interchangeable with the subject; it shows the essence of the subject. Otherwise it is a *property*. If, without being the definition, it constitutes an element in the definition, it is a genus ("this [man] is an animal"); if not, it is an *accident* ("This man is in a sitting position"). Aristotle now defines *premiss*, *problem*, and *thesis* in dialectic. A *premiss* is a question (this is extraordinary: he means "answer"), which commends itself to everyone, the majority, or informed opinion (104a8). A *problem* is an investigation of practical or theoretical importance on which there is no agreed opinion. A *thesis* is a paradoxical opinion held by a famous thinker, or at least defensible by argument if not by authority. Not all problems and theses are worth discussing. Dialectical argument uses reasoning, as explained, and induction, and Aristotle gives an excellent example of inductive argument: "If the expert pilot is the dominant pilot, and the expert driver the dominant driver, then it follows universally that the expert in any field is the best." (105a13)

Those are the preliminaries, and they constitute the most valuable part of *Topics;* the rest largely became outmoded with his own discovery of the syllogism. Yet we are reminded, as so often, not merely of Aristotle's towering genius, but of his sheer normalcy. We do often discuss subjects without an intimate grasp of first principles, and Aristotle's aim is to help us do this effectively. Aristotle is a realist: breadth of culture does not mean omniscience; correspondingly, the fact that we are not omniscient need not deter us from having wide-ranging interests; one recalls the old definition of a scholar as "one who knows something about everything and everything about something."

First, however, is an almost Empsonian discussion of ambiguities and their detection (106a1): (a) We may note that a word has more than one opposite, e.g., *sharp* has *flat* of a musical note, but *blunt* of an arrow; (b) a word and its opposite may be used in more than one field, e.g., *clear* and *dim* (Aristotle says *white* and *black*) of sound and color; (c) an opposite may be found in one field but not in another, e.g., *love* has *hate* as a mental activity, but no opposite as a physical activity; (d) an intermediate between opposites may offer a clue, e.g., *clear* and *dim* have *gray* of color but nothing of sound; (e) an ambiguity in the opposite may reveal an ambiguity in the original, e.g., *I can't see* may be *I am blind* or *I can't discern a particular object,* and this reveals a similar ambiguity in *see;* (f) privation and presence of states may offer a clue, e.g., *to possess sensation and to lack sensation* are used physiologically and psychologically; (g) derivative and grammatical inflections help, e.g., *justly* may show an ambiguity in *just;* (h) predicative uses show ambiguity, e.g., *the food is good, his character is good;* (i) genera reveal ambiguity, e.g., in Greek as in English, *donkey* may be an animal or an engine; (j) so do the genera of the opposite; (k) composite phrases containing the term show difference of usage; (l) sometimes there is ambiguity of definition; (m) comparison (Can you say "This note is sharper than that arrow"?); (n) examination of the points of difference.

Not all is as interesting as this. The second and third books deal with accident, the fourth and fifth with genus and property, the sixth and the first part of the seventh with definition. Much of the discussion is designed for clearing away loose thinking from our mind and that of our interlocutor. But not all. Aristotle is not averse from recommending his students to play on ambiguities to the end of victory in argument (110a23), or using sophistical methods to lead an opponent into making a readily refuted assertion (111b32). J. B. Morton once described logic as "an unfair means sometimes used to win an argument"; Aristotle knew all about that.

There is a substantial discussion of genus in its relation to species (120b12 ff). A genus must be predicated of all members of the same species, e.g., if some pleasures are not good, good cannot be a genus of pleasure. Next, it must belong to the essence of its subject, e.g., snow is not essentially white; white is not a genus of snow. Further, genus and species must pertain to the same category; white and snow do not; for one is a substance, the other OF WHAT KIND. Also, the genus is broader than the species; it follows that if the species is predicated, the genus must be also; and similarly that if a genus is predicated, some one of its species must be. The genus of all things not specifically different is the same; if a species falls under more than one genus, one genus must include the other. All higher genera belong to the category of essence. The definition of the genus will inevitably suit its members. But care is needed. The differentia is not the genus; it answers OF WHAT KIND? The differentia must not be placed inside the genus ("odd" is not a number) nor for that matter, inside the species. Still less must the genus be placed inside the differentia or inside the species. The genus is prior to the species and inseparable from the species. No member of a genus can share in anything contrary to that genus, e.g., if the soul (*psyche*) participates in life, and number does not, the soul cannot be number. Finally, loose language is to be avoided in logical analysis, e.g., species should not be used loosely in place of genus; and metaphorical language is especially dangerous. Some of this is tedious; much is repetitive; most is commonsense; yet someone had to make the basic analysis, and Aristotle was the first to do so.

As an example of Aristotle's sophistry we may take the passage on how to deal with complex definitions (150a1 ff). Suppose our opponent defines justice as self-discipline combined with courage. If we find two people, one self-disciplined and cowardly, the other intemperate and brave, they will be both just and unjust. Again, suppose our opponent defines a house as made up of bricks and mortar, without stating how it is made up; bricks and mortar need to be put together in a particular way to make a house. Suppose he defines courage as daring plus right opinion, it is easy to show that a man who is daring in committing crime and holds right opinions about health is not courageous. If we cannot attack his definition as a whole we should subvert it piecemeal. Better still to make our own definition!

In general the most useful of these stock methods Aristotle calls inflections and words with a common root (154a12). Inflections refer to grammatical inflection but include a wider range of relation, e.g., if justice is defined as courage, then "justly" must be equivalent to "courageously." "Words with a common root" is self-explanatory; the principle of investigation is the same. The examination of opposites is also useful.

In the last book Aristotle recapitulates the methods of dialectical reasoning. The dialectician covers the same ground as the philosopher but organizes his material differently. Aristotle discusses the best way to frame questions, the use of premisses and induction, the method of answering objections. It is difficult to attack well-established first principles, and loose definitions and metaphorical language are often ineluctable. Turning to the most effective method of defending a thesis against questioning, Aristotle makes the very pertinent point that we ought to question our own theses (160b14). To defend a thesis we must understand methods of attack. For instance, a false argument must be attacked at its point of falsity; this is the only cogent way of preventing a point being established. But we can check an objector less legitimately by questioning his questions, objecting to his objections or simply filibustering. But to answer an argument is not always to convince its exponent; we may have to argue *ad hominem,* though never contentiously. It is important, though, to look at the reasoning of the objection and to show that the conclusion is not valid, or is irrelevant, or proceeds from faulty premisses, or the like. An argument is self-evident, if it does not depend on mere opinion, if the conclusions follow necessarily from the premisses, and if it leaves no questions to be asked (162a35). An argument is fallacious if it has not reached any conclusion, if it has not reached the right conclusion, if it has followed an inappropriate method, or if it is based on false premisses (although it is possible to reach a true conclusion from false premisses: Aristotle does not give an example, but we might adduce: All lions are graminivorous; all cows are lions; therefore all cows are graminivorous). Finally, Aristotle recommends the young debater to practise converting arguments, to examine minutely the pros and cons of any thesis, to be familiar with the usual arguments; it is better to use inductive arguments against younger opponents, deductive against older; and it is dangerous to engage in argument with all and sundry when it is liable to get out of hand.

VI *Fallacious Reasoning*

It cannot be said that mankind would be much poorer if *Topics* had not survived. There is however an interesting little appendix, entitled *Sophistical Refutation.* It is a study of fallacious reasoning, and in its way it has been a work of some influence. Aristotle divides fallacies into those which are linguistic and those which are logical. Linguistic fallacies are: equivocation, or the ambiguity of a single word; ambiguity in sentence structure (as in bad poems even in English: "Still warm remembrance friendship craves"[14]—which is subject and which object?); ambiguity in composition (the famous example is "A man is capable of walking while sitting"); the wrong grouping of words ("Five is two and three"; therefore "Five is two" and "Five is three"); false accent (a technical Greek matter, but we distinguish cóntent, noun, from contént, adjective); and false inference from grammatical form (e.g., all verbs do not denote actions). Logical fallacies are slightly more complex.[15] They comprise: confusion of substance and accident (If Coriscus is other than Socrates and Socrates is a man, it does not follow that Coriscus is other than a man); confusion of absolute and relative uses (If an Indian is black all over and white of tooth, he is both white and not white); *ignoratio elenchi,* that is, not recognizing the conditions of refutation; *petitio principii,* assuming the thesis you are setting out to prove, or proving it by means of premisses which depend upon it; simple conversion of a proposition which does not admit it (to see a yellow object and say "That's honey" is to convert "All honey is yellow" illegitimately into "All yellow things are honey"; it will be observed that the line between legitimate induction and illegitimate conversion is not easy to draw); faulty reasoning back to a premiss, when the falsity of a conclusion is used to refute a premiss from which it was not in fact derived; misleading questions (had he known it, Aristotle would have enjoyed "Have you stopped beating your wife?"). The whole discussion is an interesting glimpse into the educational controversies of the age. It is also a considerable testimony to Aristotle's acumen. For though his classification, as he himself admits, is not definitive, he has in fact identified the principal fallacies by which we go astray in our own reasoning, apart altogether from misleading others.

Aristotle's logic was of cardinal importance both historically and in its own right. Russell showed ill judgment when he singled out in his so-called *History* those points with which he disagreed, and dismissed them as "wholly false, with the exception of the formal theory of the syllogism, which is unimportant." Aristotle's logic has obvious defects by modern standards. Preoccupied with the relation between propositions, he never comes to grips with the proposition itself. He is misled by the accidental forms of Greek grammar and syntax. More, he is torn between rationalism and empiricism. His search for necessary truth comes up against the brick wall of his belief in the solid "thisness" of the material world; his empiricism stops short of accepting the rule of contingency. But modern logicians other than Russell have evaluated him more justly and have seen the importance of his emphasis on formal principles. This remains his greatest achievement.

CHAPTER 4

Philosophy of Nature

ARISTOTLE'S work in natural philosophy comprises four treatises: *Physics, On the Heavens, On Coming-to-be and Passing-away,* and *Meteorology.* There is an additional work *On the Cosmos,* which is an amalgam of Aristotelian and Stoic thought, and which may safely be dated somewhere around the start of the Christian era. Fascinating as it is, it does not concern us here.

I "Physics"

Physics, as we have it, comprises eight books, which fall into two sharply differentiated halves, referred to by Aristotle himself as *On Nature* and *On Movement* respectively. The title *Physics* is something of a misnomer, or at least the meaning of the word has changed. The Greek word *physis* means "nature," and this indicates far more clearly the scope of Aristotle's treatise; we might call it *Natural Science.* Furthermore, *physis* is derived from a root expressing growth. From other sources we may say that natural science studies that which is capable of movement and involved in movement; it studies principles, but it studies them not abstractly but insofar as they are inherent in the material world (*Met.* 6, 1025b26; 11, 1061b6).

Scientific knowledge consists in the grasp of first principles. Scientific procedure passes from the familiar to the fundamental. There will either be one first principle or more than one. If one, it will be either immobile (the paradoxical position of Parmenides and the Eleatics) or subject to movement (the Ionian monists, as Thales or Anaximenes); if more than one, they will be finite in number (Empedocles) or infinite (Democritus). Aristotle is concerned to reject the Eleatic position. He may seem to us to be unduly preoccupied with it, but it would be hard to exaggerate the impact of Parmenides and Zeno on Greek thought; they seemed to set a TRESPASSERS WILL BE PROSECUTED sign across the path of natural science. Aristotle takes the Eleatic bull by the horns of its dilemma and boldly asserts that to contend that reality is a single motionless (and so unchanging) whole is to subvert all natural philosophy. He treats it as axiomatic that at least some things existing by nature are involved with motion and change and is prepared to make an induction to that effect from our ordinary experience; Aristotle's treatment of the Eleatics is not unlike G. E. Moore's treatment of the idealists. But Aristotle gives the Eleatics a run for their money and shows that in terms of his own categories "to be" has more than one meaning, thus exposing one Eleatic fallacy, and that "one" has more than one meaning. Parmenides, he holds, constructed a metaphysic out of an oversimplified syntax; and Aristotle in showing that the syntax is more complex, shows that the metaphysic is invalid.

The majority of natural philosophers posit that the first principles are contraries: rare and dense, full and void, being and nonbeing, up and down, before and behind, straight and curved, and the like. This passage alone makes it hard to understand why so many historians of philosophy write as if "the contraries" in early Greek thought mean hot and cold, wet and dry, and no others.[1] The opposites or contraries fulfill two necessary conditions of first principles: they are not generated from one another or from anything else, and everything else is derived from them. But Aristotle goes on to show that there must be three first principles. An infinite number would be as destructive of scientific knowledge as a single unchanging one. There must in fact be three: a substratum and a pair of contraries acting on it. Aristotle now turns, with this in mind, to his own view. When an uneducated man becomes an educated man, we have a substratum and two contraries, in a sense. We have in a resultant a product of matter and form. But there is a third element in the total process: this is the earlier privation of the form. In other words, in change privation is replaced by form in a substratum. Nothing comes into being from nothing; it is generated from privation in a substratum. Aristotle is expressing verbally the symbolic formula X (NOT A) $\longrightarrow$ X (A). This concept of privation—a curious one which recurs from time to time in Aristotle—fascinated him, but it was hardly an integral part of his thought, and he occasionally does fantastic things with it. He develops the same pattern of thought more fruitfully in the ninth book of *Metaphysics* through the use of potentiality and actuality.[2]

The second book of *Physics* is one of Aristotle's most important writings; it stands alongside the first as a treatment of first principles but is seemingly independent of it. He begins by seeking a definition of "nature" and "natural." Natural objects are those which have an internal source of motion; they comprise animals and their parts, plants, and the simple bodies, earth, air, fire and water. Some have claimed that nature is to be found in matter; bury a wooden bed, and wood may sprout, but a bed will not! Aristotle takes the view that nature is form not matter, for nature is more appropriately applied to the actual than to the potential, and in natural generation (in Aristotle's favorite illustration) "man begets man." He goes on to establish the difference between physics (or natural philosophy) and mathematics, which studies the same objects in a different way. (The Platonists claimed that it studied different objects.) The physicist or natural philosopher is concerned with both form and matter; his subject is form em-mattered.

There follows perhaps the most celebrated part of *Physics*, the doctrine of the four causes. Aristotle's own summary is so clear that we may present it in a slightly abbreviated version of his own words (194b23): "Cause means (a) the persistent factor out of which a thing comes into being, e.g., bronze of a statue, silver of a cup; (b) the form or blueprint, e.g., of the octave number in general and the ratio 2:1 in particular, or again the parts of a definition; (c) the immediate origin of change or rest, e.g., a man who gives advice, the father of a child; (d) the end or purpose, e.g., health is the cause of taking a walk." Aristotle notes that we can apply this last formula to activities, e.g., dieting or to material objects, e.g., surgical instruments. This is important. It is a useful, indeed essential, part of our understanding of deliberate activities and of manufactured objects alike; Aristotle extends it to all activities and all objects, and takes a thoroughly teleological view of nature. Most modern scientists reject the question "Why?" and concentrate on the question "How?" though it is significant that a student of animal behavior like Tinbergen finds the question "Why?" continually pressing upon him, for a student of animal behavior is what Aristotle basically was. But it is difficult to derive the doctrine from biology, and though Aristotle has biology in his mind, it is more likely that he derived the scheme from technical skills and applied it to biology by analogy. This is suggested by his illustrations from the sculptor and silversmith, the architect and musician, the expert adviser, and the doctor. Aristotle's isolation of four causes is of genuine importance. We incline to concentrate on the material and efficient causes, but in considering, for example, the motion of billiard balls on a table we shall not achieve much unless we look at certain mathematical patterns of angles, or understand the rules of the game. The formal and final causes are needed. Aristotle proceeds to make some detailed distinctions, for example, between essential and accidental factors. Essentially, a sculptor is the cause of a statue, but incidentally that sculptor is Polyclitus; he is also a man; he is also an animal. All these, particular and general, are properly causes; we may even speak of Polyclitus-the-sculptor. But we may also say that a white man caused the statue; the statement is true, but only by accident.

There follows a discussion of chance or luck (*tyche*). It is important to remember that Aristotle did not have mechanistic determinism as a permanent part of his philosophic scene. He is not contrasting chance with determinism, but chance with teleology, and in such a way that chance comes close to physical determinism. This is especially true in his, as in Plato's, attitude to the Atomists. It is irregular, precisely because it is not purposive. Luck in Aristotle falls under the heading of final cause, but accidentally not essentially, and is applicable only to beings capable of rational choice. In other words, luck acts as a cause where an event could have been purposively intended, but in fact was not. A man goes to shop and runs into one of his debtors. Had he known the debtor was there, he might have gone to find him. In fact, he did not know, so that his act was purposive in quality without being truly purposive. Chance has a wider extension to inanimate objects, as with the stool which chances to fall on its feet as if waiting to be sat upon. On the whole, this is a good doctrine of good luck, a bad doctrine of bad luck, explicable only in terms of the simulation of hostile purpose; but it will be observed that all this depends on a teleological approach.

This teleological approach is further emphasized as Aristotle stresses that the natural philosopher is concerned with all four causes. But three of them often coincide. It is relatively easy to see how this is true of the formal and final causes: in artifacts the form is defined by the purpose, as with a knife whose purpose is to cut, a chair designed to be sat on, a house to be lived in; and in nature form and matter are related as end and means. The equation of the efficient cause with the others is harder; Aristotle's favorite example is from natural generation, "Man begets man," the parent providing alike the efficient cause and the form. Aristotle is insistent on the final cause in nature; nature works for an end. It cannot be too strongly reiterated that for Aristotle regularity implies purpose. He does not use the machine analogy; if he did, he would use it teleologically, in terms of the mind, which designed the machine for an end. For him regularity, purpose, and design are set against chance and necessity.

The next four books deal with motion; the third and fourth are seemingly earlier than the fifth and sixth. Movement, which Aristotle equates broadly with change, and treats as a philosopher rather than as a physicist, is the actualization of a potentiality; it is a process, e.g., the movement or process of building takes place while the bricks-and-mortar are being translated into the house they are capable of becoming, not while they are standing waiting to be moved, nor after the house is complete. It will be noticed that the movement, change, or process takes place alike in the agent and the object; the builder also actualizes his potentiality in the act of building.

The remainder of the third book deals with the infinite. Aristotle's treatment is not wholly clear. It must be remembered that Greek thought generally is dominated by the thought of limit. This may be seen in the contrast between the organic completeness of a Greek temple and the capacity of a Gothic cathedral to absorb endless additions and changes of style, in the similar contrast between Greek and Shakespearean tragedy, in the very fact of the city-state. In Pythagoras limit is good, unlimited bad. In Plato (and much of this part of *Physics* is close to Plato) the world is formed by the stamping of limit, represented by the Forms, upon the unlimited, i.e., matter. So with Aristotle the infinite is potential not actual, and a privation is not a perfection. Aristotle makes some difficult distinctions between various meanings of infinite; the most important is the distinction between infinity obtained by addition and infinity obtained by division (204a6), and as Ross succinctly points out, Aristotle holds that number is infinite in the former sense, space in the latter, and time in both. To put it differently, number has a minimum but no maximum, space a maximum but no minimum. Aristotle believes firmly in the finitude of the universe.

With this behind him he can go on to the discussion of place and time. Place exists; one body can dis-place another; place is independent of either of the bodies concerned. Place not merely exists; it is functional. Aristotle, never having heard of Einstein, regards up and down, forward and backward, right and left, as absolute terms (though they may be used relatively), and the simple bodies (earth, water, air, fire) as having appropriate natural movements. Yet place is difficult to define. It is not a body, or two bodies would be coincident. It is not form or matter. Form or shape is the boundary of the object; place the boundary of that which contains the object. Matter is a *what,* place is a *where.* Nor can we say that place is in place; in any fundamental sense a thing cannot be in itself. Place is not an interval between the extremities of that which circumscribes an object, for this exists accidentally, not permanently and independently. We are then left with the view that the place of a body is the innermost, unmoved boundary of that which circumscribes it at the point of contact (212a20). Aristotle in fact rejects the Newtonian construct of space as a kind of infinite room, and in making of space a relationship between body and its environment, comes close to the general Theory of Relativity. Solomon Bochner accords Aristotle's treatment of place high praise, calling it original and modern, and points out that Aristotle is really anticipating the distinction between laboratory space and cosmological space.[3]

Aristotle's next subject is *void.* He begins, as usual, with a survey of previous views. Void is regarded as place with nothing in it, place deprived of body. Aristotle refutes the arguments for void based on the impossibility of motion without it, and on differences of density within bodies. His own argumentation is complex and outmoded, as where it depends on the natural movement of simple bodies. One argument is of historic importance. He maintains that velocity depends: (1) on the resistance of the medium, and (2) on the weight of the body. But in void there is no resistance. No matter what their weights, all bodies should pass through void in an equal time, in fact no time at all. This is a contradiction. The historic importance is that Galileo understood Aristotle to mean that a heavy body would move faster through void than a lighter one. Hence, the Pisa experiments as a test and the whole story of post-Renaissance dynamics. Differences of density within bodies Aristotle explains in terms of his own philosophy of potentiality and actuality; the size of a sensible body can expand or contract because it is potentially large or small. Void is thus for Aristotle an unnecessary hypothesis.

Time is not identical with movement, but it is not independent of it; Aristotle uses a Rip Van Winkle illustration to show that our awareness of time and awareness of change go together. Time is associated with our awareness of before and after, of two nows with an interval between them. Time is the number of movement in relation to before and after (219b2). To watch movement in space is to be aware of a succession of heres; to observe movement in time is to be aware of a succession of nows; but we are not to think of points in space or time as irreducible units. To be in time is to be measurable by time. Does time depend on conscious life (*psyche*)? This fascinating question Aristotle answers, a trifle hesitantly, by saying that a definition could be found which would apply in such circumstances; what would be lacking would be awareness of time. He concludes that time is the measure of all kinds of motion or change, but primarily of locomotion, and primarily of motion in a circle. One feels that he would approve of the design of clocks and watches. Bochner again is loud in praise of this section of Aristotle's work, commenting on his sheer merit as a physicist. He singles out five of Aristotle's assertions: (1) time is the determinant of motion or change; (2) time can be expressed mathematically as a linear continuum; (3) time can be measured only by periodic events; (4) the unity of the universe is linked with the unity of time; (5) there can be no awareness of time without a perceiving mind.[4] The last two have been fully assimilated only by twentieth-century physics.

In the fifth book we deal with different types of change or movement: some of the material recurs in the eleventh book of *Metaphysics*. Changes are of three kinds: accidental, partial, and essential. Change considered as movement or process may also be divided into qualitative change, quantitative change, and locomotion. Substance is not subject to movement in this way. Aristotle adds that there is no change of change or movement of movement (but this is doubtful: what about acceleration as a change of velocity?). Now follows an excellent section of clear distinctions. To be *together* is to be in one place, *apart* in different places. Things are *in contact* when their extremities are together. *Between* implies at least three terms. To be *in succession* is to be after a beginning, without a between; it may be applied to position, form, or other respects. *Contiguity* implies *succession* and *contact*. *Continuity* is a subdivision of *contiguity;* it implies that two objects have identical boundaries of contact. This section is a vital prelude to the sixth book, and is the most important part of the fifth book. The remainder discusses unity and diversity of movement, contrary movements, and movement and rest as natural and as induced by outside forces. Aristotle's view that fire has a natural movement up and earth a natural movement down handicapped physical science for centuries. In general the fifth book seems, and is, slighter than the other books; it is best treated as a prologue to the second part.

The sixth book, with its discussion of continuity of movement, is another matter. Continuity implies infinite divisibility, and we must not think of a continuum of space as made up of indivisible points, or a continuum of time of indivisible moments. This simple assertion, which Aristotle defends by commonsensical considerations, enables him to challenge the paradoxes of Parmenides's disciple Zeno. He first uses an argument similar to Zeno's to show the infinite divisibility of time and space. Simply: if A is swifter-moving than B, it travels over a longer distance in the same time. To travel the same distance as B it will take less long, but during that time B will have travelled a shorter distance still, and so *ad infinitum*. So, both the distance and the time are infinitely divisible. He then turns to Zeno. Zeno asserted that it was impossible to traverse an infinitely divisible finite space in a finite length of time. Not so, says Aristotle, since the finite length of time is itself infinitely divisible. This is masterly argumentation.

The present, the "now," is indivisible, the limit of past and future, and nothing can be in motion, or for that matter at rest, in it. Everything that changes must be divisible; a movement is divisible both in relation to the time of the movement, and to the movement of its parts. In such a process of change there is no absolute point of departure, but there is a moment, a "now," when we can say that the change has taken place. This is directed against a sophistic argument suggesting that Dion could not have died either when he was alive or when he was dead. Primary time thus relates to a completion of change, not a beginning. "Thus, what has changed must have been changing, and what is changing must have changed; changing is preceded by having changed, and having changed by changing; and we can never take one stage and say that it is absolutely the first" (237b3). So Aristotle, developing his theme, in Ross's words, with "unwearied diligence" and "unfailing accuracy," gradually returns to Zeno.[5] He denies that anything can take an infinite time to perform a finite movement, or can perform an infinite movement in a finite time, and after a discussion of rest, gives a more systematic exposition and refutation of Zeno's four famous fallacies: (a) that it is impossible to cross a racecourse, because there is a midpoint to reach, and a further midpoint, and so on to infinity, and it is impossible to traverse an infinite number of points in a finite time; (b) the "Achilles": that a fast runner cannot catch a slow runner, for when he reaches the point the other was at, the other has moved on, and so *ad infinitum,* (c) the arrow: an object is at rest when it occupies a space equal to itself; this is true at any moment in the flight of an arrow; therefore the moving arrow is at rest; (d) that if masses B and C move in opposite directions past a mass A equal to themselves, B moves twice as fast past C as past A and thus is moving twice as fast as itself. We have already noted Aristotle's refutation of the first, and his denial that a continuum of time can be divided into moments; on the last he rightly distinguishes between relative motions. At the end of the book Aristotle denies infinite change; the only eternal motion he allows is simple motion in a circle.

The seventh book creates a number of problems.[6] It was ignored by Eudemus; it breaks the sequence otherwise to be found in books 5, 6, and 8, and its opening chapters exist in two different versions. On the other hand it contains some quite casual references to earlier parts of *Physics,* so that it does fit in some kind of sequence. We must think of Aristotle continually revising his lectures; either this is an independent short course, inserted by later editors because of its subject matter, or it is part of an earlier conclusion to the course, which was superseded by book 8. The two openings may have been used by Aristotle at different times, or they may have been different students' notes, or one may be Aristotle's lecture notes and the other the work of a student. But in view of the nature of the book a brief summary will suffice. Everything that is in movement must be moved by something.

But an infinite regress is not possible. We must call a halt; there must be a first cause of movement and a first recipient of movement (243a27). The proximate mover and the thing it moves must always be in contact; there can be nothing mediate between them. Everything that is altered in quality is altered by perceptible agents, and such alteration takes place in perceptible objects. The rest of the book consists of a lengthy discussion of whether a valid comparison can be made between different kinds of motion, e.g., circular and linear, and a briefer examination of proportional forces.

With the eighth book we are back in the mainstream of the course, but we also find ourselves in a world of lofty conclusions, reminiscent of the twelfth book of *Metaphysics*, and we are aware that here is one of the most carefully presented series of arguments in all of Aristotle. We have seen that movement exists. Aristotle now shows that it must be eternal; for if there was a first movement there must have been something capable of producing it and something capable of experiencing it, and these must have either come into being or changed from a static to a dynamic condition; either involves a movement before the "first" movement. There never was a time in the past without movement, nor will there be in the future. Aristotle poses and counters some objections to his thesis and passes to his next step. Either everything is permanently at rest (Parmenides), or everything is permanently in motion (Heraclitus and his followers), or some things are in motion and others at rest. If it is the last, either some things are permanently in motion and others permanently at rest, or everything is sometimes in motion, sometimes at rest, or some things are permanently at rest and others permanently in motion and others vary. The last alone solves all the problems. The next step is to show, a little speciously, that movement must be due to some agent. Movement is of three kinds. A living creature has within itself its source of movement; it is moved by nature. An inanimate object may be moved in accordance with the natural motion of the elements, or contrary to them. The latter plainly requires an agent; for the former, Aristotle actually identifies two agents, one which made them light and heavy in the first place, and the other which helps them realize their nature by removing obstacles to their natural movement. Aristotle is now ready to establish that the prime mover (i.e., that which ultimately brings about movement in other things) must be either self-moved or unmoved (256a4 ff.), since otherwise there is an infinite regress. Of these alternatives he argues that it is unmoved. His basic argument is from analogy. It is not necessary to be acted upon in order to act: a teacher does not have to be a learner, a pitcher need not himself be pitched (257a3), nor a builder built. He proceeds to dismiss the idea of a self-mover, who would either as a whole move himself as a whole or with one part of himself move the other. The former would involve the mover being both potentially and actually in motion at the same time; the latter would mean that the part not the whole was the real self-mover, and would reduce the prime mover to a combination of an unmoved mover and a part which receives movement without causing it. In other words, the concept of the self-mover reduces itself to an unmoved mover in any event.

There may be more than one prime mover. (This and two similar passages are probably late additions and refer to the doctrine of Callippus, which recurs in *Metaphysics* 12.) *The* prime mover, the all-encompassing origin of being and continuous change (259a3) must be single, eternal, and unmoved. The mover imparts to some things an eternal movement; other things are subject to alternation between movement and rest because they are moved by a moving mover. Aristotle at this point makes what he calls a fresh start (260a20). He has so far assumed a fundamental eternal continuous movement; he now shows that this is possible. The primary form of movement is locomotion. Further, all other forms of movement pass from one opposite to another; they are bounded by limits and cannot be eternal. But there is a form of motion which can be simple, continuous, and infinite, and that is circular locomotion. Aristotle argues this at some length and then returns to his doctrine of the prime mover. He shows that the prime mover is without parts and without magnitude; for (a) a finite magnitude cannot produce eternal movement, (b) a finite magnitude cannot have infinite power, and (c) an infinite magnitude cannot have a finite power (266a10 ff). It will be noticed that Aristotle, not having studied under Newton, assumes that continuous motion can be produced only by the continuous application of force. The eternal movement of the heavens then must be produced by a being without magnitude and without parts. The mover must be situated at one of the two key points, the center or the circumference, and since the outermost spheres rotate the fastest, the mover must be at the circumference. Aristotle does not ask how an incorporeal first principle can move a physical body and ends his lectures with a solid reassertion: "The prime mover produces a motion which is eternal and extends through infinite time. So it is clear that the mover is indivisible, without parts, possessing no magnitude" (267b24). It is important to note that he always speaks of the mover as neuter, never as masculine.

Physics is of uneven value, and must have seemed so even in Aristotle's own day. At its best, as in the second book or parts of the sixth, it is of outstanding brilliance. Some of it is tedious and irrelevant. What remains impressive is the way Aristotle builds—on the views of his predecessors, critically treated, and his own observations of the natural world—a mighty series of generalizations, culminating in a theological vision. Few scientists are prepared to let their system expand beyond the interpretation of sense-data to the interpretation of their interpretations; few theologians have their thinking so closely rooted in the facts of science that their theology is the natural outcome of a course of scientific lectures.

II "On the Universe"

On the Universe[7] is perhaps the proper translation of the work more familiarly known as *On the Heavens* (*De Caelo*): the name in any case does not go back to Aristotle. Aristotle's universe had the earth at the center; at the perimeter was the sphere of the fixed stars; and in between were the spheres carrying the planets. The first two books, which are by far the most substantial, treat the outer spheres; the last two, which are slighter, treat the sublunary regions. Aristotle begins by asserting that natural science is broadly concerned with bodies and magnitudes and their motions and the way they are affected, and with the first principles involved (268a1). After these preliminaries he argues that there is such a thing as simple motion, that circular motion is simple, and that simple motion is basically the motion of a simple body; further, circular motion, being complete (not needing a reverse motion to return to the starting point), is primary. Circular motion (which we see in the sky) is not the natural motion of any of the four "simple bodies" (earth, air, fire, and water). There must therefore be in the universe a fifth element (or quintessence), of which the heavens are formed, whose nature it is to move in a circle. This primary body Aristotle calls *aether*. It has no weight or lightness (since these are a tendency to move towards or away from the center); it is ungenerated and indestructible (since this arises from opposition, and circular motion has no opposite); it is eternal, unaging, changeless, impassible. Aristotle is strangely concerned to prove that circular motion has no opposite, and in attempting to do so uses one of his famous phrases "God and nature produce nothing to no purpose" (271a33). Next, he maintains at some length that an infinite body cannot exist; he uses a miscellany of logical and mathematical arguments to show this. Nor can there be more than one universe; this is directed against the atomists Leucippus and Democritus, who held the contrary; this too is argued at length, mainly on grounds of natural motions and natural places. Finally, the universe did not have a beginning and will not pass away. Aristotle's treatment of this is characteristic. He reviews summarily past theories and dismisses the possibility that the universe had a beginning but will have no end. The view that there is alternate dissolution and combination of the elements in fact involves an eternal world in a process of change. Generation and destruction of the universe, if it is the only one, is impossible, since this would require preexistent matter and a reversion to that state. He goes on to a careful examination of the terms involved and concludes with a succession of extremely convoluted arguments in defense of the proposition that the universe is eternal.

After a recapitulation of this proposition Aristotle in the second book asks whether the sphere of the heavens has a top and bottom, left and right, and concludes that what is natural to the lower stages of animal life must be natural to the universe; he is aware of, but dismisses, the difficulty of applying this to a sphere. So much for relativity!

Now comes what Ross properly termed one of Aristotle's "boldest essays in *a priori* construction." [8] Aristotle seeks to demonstrate why the universe is as it is. The activity of a god is eternal life, with the consequence that the divine must be in eternal motion (286a9).

It will be noticed that this makes the outermost heaven divine and asserts that divinity involves eternal motion. This on the face of it is a very different picture from that of the Unmoved Mover and has led some scholars to regard references to the Unmoved Mover in this work as later interpolations. The conclusion, however, is not assured, since, as the early commentator Simplicius is at pains to say, Aristotle is here speaking of a divine *body*. The heavens must be spherical, since they can be observed to revolve, and since the sphere is the primary shape. Then, as occasionally happens, Aristotle warms with wonder: "This demonstrates that the universe is spherical, and turned with such precision that nothing made by hand or visible to the eye is remotely comparable. None of the elements composing it is capable of receiving such smooth precision as the nature of the outer envelope: to take a parallel, the more distant elements stand as water to earth" (287b15). He goes on to the direction and regularity of the revolution of the universe (rather oddly suggesting at one point that a missile has its maximum speed in mid-flight) (288a20). Next follows the composition of the stars, not fire but the fifth element, and their immobility relative to their own sphere (which carries them round). Aristotle dismisses the Pythagorean doctrine of the harmony of the spheres: not merely is the harmony inaudible, but the noise would be indescribably shattering if it existed. The stars are spherical: Nature produces nothing irrationally or to no end (291b14), and the sphere is ill adapted to locomotion having no "lead in." This is an a priori argument, but when Aristotle turns to the moon he uses observation, both of the apparent shape of the moon when not at the full, and the shadow of moon on sun during an eclipse. There is a similar observation of the passage of the moon between Mars and the earth; this can be dated to May 4, 357 B.C. at about 9 P.M. (292a5). An important, and truly scientific, passage criticizes the Pythagoreans for forcing their account of phenomena into line with their preconceived theories: theories should be derived from the phenomena (293a25). The great scheme concludes with the earth, spherical in shape, (again there is observation of lunar eclipses and the different apparent position of stars from different viewpoints supporting a priori arguments: 297b24), and at rest in the center. Aristotle's estimate of the circumference is about 45,000 miles, which is nearly twice the true figure; the straits of Gibraltar, he suggests somewhat contradictorily, may not be too far from India across the Atlantic (298a9); it was this which encouraged Columbus.

With the third book we turn to the sublunary regions, and Aristotle starts again from first principles. He uses the word "natural" of substances or of their functions and affects. By substances he means earth, air, fire, and water and the fifth element, and the things composed of them, e.g., the whole universe and its parts, or again animals, plants, and their parts; by affects and functions, he means such things as their movements, changes, transformations into one another. The study of nature—physical research—is concentrated on bodies or objects with extension.[9] It is a seminal passage.

He has dealt with the first element: he goes on to *two* remaining elements (298b7). We expect four, but he distinguishes them by weight or lightness, and by this criterion water is subsumed under earth, air under fire. The rest of the book is an extended examination and refutation of the views of his predecessors. He rejects the a priori system of Melissus and Parmenides, who disbelieved in change; the theory of continual flux that he attributes to Heraclitus; the use of numbers as material principles, as held by some Pythagoreans; the atoms and void of Leucippus and Democritus; the "seeds" of Anaxagoras, which are substances like flesh and bone, which are homoeomerous (i.e., "like-parted" or uniform, so that when divided they remain flesh and bone and do not divide into more basic elements); all monistic views, which would reduce the world to a single element; and the complex theories of Plato in *Timaeus,* to which he constantly returns. He has more sympathy for Empedocles, who did believe that the elements were earth, air, fire, and water. Aristotle's own position is that an element is "that into which other bodies are analysed, being inherent in them potentially or actually, but which cannot itself be analysed into further elements different in kind" (302a12). The elements cannot be infinite in number but there must be more than one. They are in fact in the sublunary region earth, air, fire, and water. These cannot be eternal, since they can be observed to dissolve (304b26). They come into being and can only come into being out of each other. One other passage here is of some importance. It deals with motion. The origin of motion lies in nature when it is internal, force when external (301b18). All movement is either natural or enforced; force can accelerate natural movement and is the total explanation of unnatural movement.

Finally, in the fourth book he deals with weight and lightness, and reiterates that "heavy" and "light" are ways of expressing a capacity for natural motion; they allude to a tendency toward the center or toward the periphery. Weight and lightness are often relative terms, but they have an absolute use, and we may legitimately speak in an absolute sense of "up" and "down." Of the four elements fire is absolutely light, air relatively light, water relatively heavy, earth absolutely heavy. Shape does not cause motion, but it may contribute to acceleration or deceleration. On this curious note, and on a criticism of Democritus, the treatise ends. Yet the question why a flat piece of metal floats and a smaller and less heavy piece of a different shape sinks, is in fact an important one, and Galileo, who added experiment to observation, disposed of it in a masterly manner.

III "On Coming-to-be and Passing-away"

On Coming-to-be and Passing-away is a fascinating little treatise. Characteristically, Aristotle starts by examining the views of his predecessors. He dismisses cursorily the monists, for whom coming-to-be and passing-away must be merely alterations of their basic substance, but he accords a fuller treatment to the pluralists—Empedocles, Anaxagoras—and especially the atomists; indeed he says they are all superficial except Democritus, and he cannot accept atomism. Aristotle distinguishes coming-to-be and passing-away from alteration, from growth and diminution, and from the composition and dissolution of a mere aggregation. Coming-to-be and passing-away may be used in an unqualified sense of substances or in a qualified sense of the other categories. In each instance there is a substrate, proximate matter, and that which comes-to-be does so out of that which does not exist, or, more precisely, out of that which exists potentially but not actually.

Aristotle then goes on to discuss matter and the elements (earth, air, fire, and water). These elements are the proximate matter of the homoeomerous bodies, that is, of bodies whose parts on division are all alike, which are, so to say, chemically compounded; these in turn form the anhomoeomerous parts of natural bodies, and so ultimately the bodies themselves. For example, blood, flesh, bone are homoeomerous; hand, foot, eye are anhomoeomerous; and all are, at different levels, parts of the human body. The elements combine to form the homoeomerous bodies, combination implies action and passion, and action and passion imply contact. The rest of the first book largely comprises definitions and explanations of these terms. Contact means juxtaposition; reciprocal contact the power of moving and being moved, that is, action and passion. It is important to observe that Aristotle allows for a contact that is not reciprocal, for a mover, which is unmoved (323a31; cf. 324a30) and has surely in mind the doctrine of the Unmoved Mover, which appears at its fullest in the twelfth book of *Metaphysics*. He proceeds, constantly with an eye on his predecessors, to action and passion, which involve the actualizing of a potentiality, in which the agent assimilates the patient to itself, e.g., fire, being hot, assimilates to itself that which is not hot but is potentially hot. Finally, he discusses combination. Anything is subject to combination, which, being readily modified in shape, is capable of acting or being acted upon and is open to combination with anything similarly open to combination. Combination is the union of things open to combination, once they have experienced alteration (328b20).

In the second book we return to the so-called elements, earth, air, fire, and water. They are not, in Aristotle's view, really elements, for they are not eternal and unchangeable. They are "changing informations[10] of primary matter, distinctively characterized by qualities that belong to certain primary contrarieties"; these contrarieties are hot and cold, wet and dry, the first pair active, the second passive. The simple bodies (as he now calls them) are characterized by these qualities in pairs, with one predominating: earth is dry (and cold), water cold (and wet), air wet (and hot), fire hot (and dry); the predominant characterization of water is odd. It will be observed that by qualities earth is the contrary of air and water of fire. None of these simple bodies is prior to the others; they all come-to-be out of each other by the change of one or both qualities; the simplest change is plainly cyclical. After some criticism of Empedocles (who took earth, air, fire, and water as his "roots") Aristotle shows how the homoeomerous bodies come-to-be out of the simple bodies by combination, and how therefore every compound body in the sublunary world is ultimately compounded of these simple bodies.

The treatise concludes with a brief discussion of causality. The material cause he describes as "the possibility of being and not-being"; "coming-to-be and passing-away must occur in the field of that which can be and not be" (335b4). The formal cause he treats only in passing, and he identifies it with the final cause, speaking specifically of three causes. The rest is a much more elaborate examination of the efficient cause. Aristotle argues that any explanation of coming-to-be (like Plato's Theory of Forms) which ignores the efficient cause is inadequate. He proceeds to identify the efficient cause of coming-to-be and passing-away with the sun's passage through the ecliptic, showing that coming-to-be is associated with the sun's approach and passing-away with its withdrawal and that this further explains the cyclical process. At this point Aristotle appears to introduce an actively creative deity: "God perfected the universe by making coming-to-be an eternal process" (336b32), but he may be writing loosely. It is important to note that he is speaking not merely of a water-air-fire-water cycle, which he cites (oddly omitting earth), but also of cycles such as man-seed-embryo-child-youth-man, which are also endlessly repeated. Finally, in an appendix he establishes that the cyclical process of coming-to-be and passing-away takes place, in every sense, of necessity.

IV "Meteorology"

Meteorology is today the least rewarding of Aristotle's works on physical science. The subject matter is unexciting, and scientific treatment has advanced so markedly that Aristotle's errors have only a slight historic interest. The work suffers from the basic defect of Greek science—the experimental technique is absent, and it does not challenge or confirm the often excellent observations. The title *Meteorology* is in a modern sense misleading. The work embraces astronomy, geography, and geology, as well as what we should call meteorology.

The most famous passage is the opening of the first book, which sets the present work in a general scheme of the sciences (a) *Physics:* first causes and natural motion; (b) *On the Heavens* 1–2: astronomy; (c) *On the Heavens* 3–4; *On Coming-to-be and Passing-away:* the four elements and their transformations, and growth and decay in general; (d) *Meteorology:* everything that happens naturally, but without perfect regularity; phenomena common to air and water; the nature and phenomena of earth; winds, earthquakes, and others; (e) the biological works dealing with animals and plants.

Aristotle first recapitulates earlier conclusions. In the sublunary sphere there are four elements: fire rises to the top with air next to it; earth sinks to the bottom with water next to it. These are the material causes of all sublunar events; the efficient cause is the movement of the celestial reason; and Aristotle embarks on a complex discussion of the place of air in the scheme of things. The rest of the first book deals with shooting stars, the Aurora Borealis, comets, the Milky Way, rain, cloud and mist, dew and frost, snow, hail, winds and rivers, climatic changes with erosion and silting. Shooting stars he attributes to inflammable exhalations from earth being set in motion as they rise by the movement of the nearest celestial sphere, or by heat being ejected downwards through condensation. He has observed that their movement is usually transverse and sublunary. The Aurora Borealis (which has been recorded for Greece) he attributes to the condensation of air. Comets are not a conjunction of planets or a rarely appearing planet; they too are caused by exhalations, or by the movement of a star. The Milky Way is formed by a similar process by the movement of a large number of stars in the region where they are thickest; this theory is of particular interest since it was to hold the floor till the time of Newton.

An important philosophic principle is involved in Aristotle's assertion that outside the field of sense-perception we must rely on possibilities; Descartes[11] took this up and made it his own, adding that the possibilities must be consistent with known phenomena. For the rest we may note Aristotle's awareness that seasonal changes are caused by the sun's movement along the ecliptic (346b46) and the extent of his geographical knowledge (350a14 ff. cf. 2, 362b12 ff). He contends that the largest rivers flow from the highest mountains. His plan is overschematic, and there are strange pieces of knowledge and strange gaps. Thus in Asia, Aristotle knows the Hindu Kush ("Parnassus": but he should have written Paropamisus) and something of the river system on both sides. He does not know the Ganges and for some strange reason does not mention the Tigris and Euphrates, of which he must have been aware. He does not know the great rivers of China at all. In Europe he does not know the Rhine or Elbe; still more strangely he does not know the Alps and derives the Danube (Ister) from the Pyrenees. In Africa he seems to know the Senegal (Chremetes). He derives this and one branch of the Nile from some mountains that he calls the Silver Mountains. This is interesting. He has perhaps a dim awareness of the Ruwenzori range. But he probably also knows of the Niger flowing from west to east; he identifies it with the main branch of the Nile, and assumes for schematic reasons that it must flow from the same range as the Senegal.

We learn more of his geographical knowledge in the second book. But first we must note his excellent observations of erosion and silting, drawn mainly from Egypt; he is aware that such changes are infinitesimally slow and that generations pass without perceptible changes. From rivers he passes to the sea and shows that its source is not like that of a river. Flow in the sea arises from contraction in a narrow space (he must have in mind the Euripus between Euboea and the mainland, where the current is continually shifting) or from differences in depth of the seabed or the inflow of rivers. This is the nearest Aristotle approaches to a comment on tides; they are of course very slight in the Mediterranean. Aristotle gives his view that water surrounds the earth, and that the saltness of the sea is due to evaporation of fresh water by the sun. It is with the treatment of winds that we learn more of Aristotle's picture of the earth. It is a sphere: elsewhere, as we have seen, he gives about 45,000 miles for its circumference.[12] It is divided into zones, two temperate zones, which are habitable, being sandwiched between the excessive heat of the equatorial zone and the excessive cold of the Arctic and Antarctic. But the habitable zone does not extend the whole way round because of the interposition of Ocean (362a32 ff). Aristotle believes that rain is caused by moist exhalations from the earth, wind by dry exhalations; he will not have it that wind is air in motion.[13] For the analysis of the several winds in relation to the points of the compass he used a diagram. Earthquakes he attributes to dry exhalations which have no outlet, thunder to the forcible ejection of dry exhalations caught in the clouds. Aristotle is obsessed with exhalations; it is to his credit that he has observed them and drawn conclusions from his observations, but once again we become aware of the failure of even the greatest Greek scientists to devise experiments with which to test their theories.

The third book continues with the theme of exhalations, which Aristotle uses to explain hurricanes, whirlwinds, and thunderbolts. He makes use of observers' reports of the destruction by fire of the famous temple of Ephesus in 356 B.C. The rest of the book deals with rainbows and similar phenomena, which Aristotle rightly attributes to reflection. His account, though not wholly accurate, is shrewd. He seems aware of prismatic effects in breaking light into colors. He regards the rainbow as three-colored—red, green, and blue; he has observed the yellow band between the red and green and explains it as an effect of the juxtaposition of contrasting colors. He makes a curious mistake in describing green as one of the painter's primary colors, not to be obtained by mixing; he should have said yellow. We unexpectedly become aware of a field in which Aristotle does not move with assurance. His mathematical demonstration that the rainbow cannot be larger than a semicircle is excellent; it involves a theorem not found in Euclid.

This concludes *Meteorology* proper. The fourth book is an independent treatise: its authenticity has been impugned by some on insufficient grounds.[14] Its subject is chemical change. Aristotle acknowledges four causal factors combined into four elements, as we have seen, fire being hot and dry, air hot and wet, water cold and wet, earth cold and dry; he regards hot and cold as active, wet and dry as passive. He considers the force of these factors in producing change, using two main analogies, the cooking of food and the ripening of fruit. Hardness and softness are related to solidification and liquefaction; this leads him to an interesting illustration from iron-working (383a32), which makes it clear that the Greeks knew but did not understand the effect of carburization through repeated reheating.

Toward the end of the book Aristotle enumerates eighteen pairs of qualities, which result from a body's chemical structure. These (with their negatives) are: liable to solidify, liable to melt, liable to soften through heat, liable to soften through water, flexible, fragile, liable to fragmentation, capable of taking an impression, plastic, liable to being squeezed, ductile, malleable, fissile, cuttable, viscous, compressible, combustible, capable of giving off fumes (385a12). Some of the distinctions are subtle but precise; to be squeezable is to contract under pressure, to be compressible is to contract into the same form; hair is ductile, stone is not, wool is ductile and squeezable, phlegm is ductile but not squeezable, sponge is squeezable but not ductile. Behind these distinctions is the important distinction between those substances Aristotle calls homoeomerous and other substances. Homoeomerous substances, as we have seen, are what we would call chemical compounds, and they in turn form anhomoeomerous bodies, organic and inorganic. Looking forward to a fuller treatment in the biological works, he concludes by asserting in physical science too the importance of the formal-final cause, though the final cause may be discerned in inverse proportion to the predominance of matter (390a3). Still "we know what and why a thing is if we grasp its matter or its formula—better still both—in relation to its coming-to-be and passing-away—together with its cause of motion." (390b17)

Aristotle's work in physical science is far inferior to his work in biology. George Henry Lewes put his finger on the weakness: "Compare the *Physics* of ARISTOTLE with the *Principia* of NEWTON. . . . In the latter we find metaphysical abstractions, but not the metaphysical Method. The formulas are gained objectively, not subjectively: they are accurate *descriptions of the observed order in phenomena;* they are moulded on realities; they were abstracted from objects, and have been rigorously *verified* according to the Ideal and Real tests. The formulas of ARISTOTLE are not more transcendental, but they want the guarantee of Verification." [15]

CHAPTER 5

Biology

TWO facts would be widely agreed. First, that it is as a biologist that Aristotle stands supreme. Second, that his biological works have been sadly neglected, since few in this fragmented age can claim expertise in both biology and Greek philosophy. No one has done for the biological works what Sir David Ross accomplished for so much of Aristotle. D'Arcy Thompson, the last of the great polymaths, did an excellent annotated translation of *Historia Animalium* in the Oxford series, and A. L. Peck has worked usefully within the compass of the Loeb series. But it remains very hard for the general reader to form a just estimate of Aristotle's work here. More serious, the general interpreters of Aristotle tend to ignore the biology; Marjorie Grene is a notable exception.

I *Classification of Animals*

Historia Animalium, often called *The History of Animals* but better entitled *Zoological Researches,* is a general introduction to zoology. The great Cuvier appraised it warmly: "I cannot read this work without being ravished with astonishment. In fact, it is impossible to conceive how a single individual could possibly have collected and compared the quantity of particular facts which are the basis of the many generalizations contained in this work, facts of which his predecessors had no idea at all." [1] Certainly the generalizations are based on a remarkable series of observations, which mainly belong to Aristotle's two years at Lesbos,[2] shortly after Plato's death, though he doubtless continued to add to them subsequently. All in all, it has been shown that Aristotle identified 495 species of animals,[3] one more than Pliny enumerated four centuries later. But many of Pliny's are traveler's tales, and Aristotle actually knew 156 species unknown to Pliny.

At the outset there has been some displacement of the text[4] The original opening was almost certainly: "Differences between animals relate to their ways of life, their activities, their habits and their parts" (487a11). These differences are exemplified, as by habitat, mode of progression, gregariousness or solitariness, diet, nocturnal habits, domestication, call, sex-behavior, disposition (some proverbial lore here!), and parts simple or composite including secondary characteristics (here we pick up the sentences which inaugurate the text as we have it). We may note in passing the excellent observation of the metamorphosis into gnats of larvae found in water (487b5). Other distinctions are drawn, of which the most important are between those animals endowed with blood and others, and between the viviparous and oviparous (489a30 ff.); his observation that the cetaceans are mammals is noteworthy. This leads him to an enumeration (it is hardly a classification) of some of the main genera: those with blood as birds, fishes, cetaceans; those without blood, as shellfish (hard-shelled and soft-shelled), mollusks, and insects. He suggests that other groups are not extensive, but it is hard to see why viviparous and oviparous quadrupeds are not among his main groups, as they are elsewhere (cf 490b32; 505b28). Man stands somewhat apart, a simple species, admitting no differentiation (490b18).

From this and other passages we can reconstruct Aristotle's natural scale:

- MAN
- OTHER ANIMALS ENDOWED WITH BLOOD AND VIVIPAROUS:
  - LAND MAMMALS
  - CETACEA
- ANIMALS ENDOWED WITH BLOOD AND OVIPAROUS
  - WITH PERFECT EGG
    - BIRDS
    - REPTILIANS
  - WITH IMPERFECT EGG
    - FISHES
- BLOODLESS ANIMALS
  - OVIPAROUS
    - CEPHALOPODS
    - CRUSTACEANS
  - LARVIPAROUS
    - INSECTS

SPONTANEOUSLY GENERATED
OTHER MOLLUSKS
INTERMEDIATE CREATURES
ASCIDIANS
HOLOTHURIA (?)
PLANTS
HIGHER
LOWER
INANIMATE MATTER

It is a remarkable vision of the unbroken chain of life.

The rest of the first book deals with the constituent parts of man (and incidentally of other viviparous blooded animals). There is little that calls for comment here; Aristotle's knowledge of internal anatomy is naturally limited, and we may content ourselves with noting his excellent observations of man's upright posture (494a27), singled out on a priori grounds but nonetheless important; his belief (perhaps based on misleading observations) that the back of the head is hollow (494b34); his curious suggestion that the heart has three cavities and his understandable ignorance of the difference between veins and arteries (496a4); and his care to observe sacrificial victims (496b25). This last is important: Aristotle is prepared to fill the gaps in his knowledge of man by analogy with other animals.

The following books continue with observations of other animals in prodigal detail; these are directed to defining the main genera of the animals endowed with blood, though specific differences are also noticed. Mistakes are made. At the outset of the second book we are told, wrongly, that the lion has but one bone in his neck (497b16): this is true of the whale and one wonders if there has been some confusion of specimens. There is a remote but vivid account of the tiger (501a25); a triple row of teeth in each jaw sounds fanciful. Some errors may be traced to the use of observation: when Aristotle says the human male has more teeth than the female (501b20), he may have observed women whose wisdom teeth have not come through. Among many admirable observations we may note his awareness that the marten and weasel have a bony penis (500b24: he is wrong about fox and wolf); his careful distinction between different teeth (501a8 ff.); his masterly description of the four chambers of the stomach of ruminants, which undoubtedly arose from dissection

(507a33 ff.). One important feature of Aristotle's classification is his concept of "doubling up" (*epamphoterizein*). He uses it when an animal seems to fit into more than one class, as apes double up between humans and quadrupeds (502a16); elsewhere we find the sea anemone doubling up between plants and animals.[5]

The third book has a particularly interesting passage, which gives an account of a labelled diagram (510a29) that once accompanied the text, illustrating the testicles of mammals. His description is detailed and evidently based on dissection. His account of blood vessels, though of considerable interest, is not satisfactory, but it is in accordance with the best medical science of his day, which he quotes at length. He is aware of the chambers of the heart, but wrongly identifies them as three; of the complexity of the blood vessels, without of course understanding the full principle of circulation; and of the relationship between fibers and coagulation (515b27). Other topics include bones, cartilage, hair, and skin (including some excellent observations of seasonal changes of plumage in birds), flesh (situated between skin and bone: 519b27), fat and suet (excellently distinguished: 520a6), marrow, milk, and semen.

In the next book similar analysis is applied to animals not endowed with blood: cephalopods, crustacea, testacea, and insects. George Henry Lewes, who tended to be critical of Aristotle's science, appraised the detailed richness and systematic nature of these chapters and noted that they show direct personal observation and a judicious estimate of the unscientific tales of fishermen.[6] An extended quotation from D'Arcy Thompson will show the quality of Aristotle's observation of cuttlefish:

> These cuttle-fishes are creatures that we seldom see, but in the Mediterranean they are an article of food and many kinds are known to the fishermen. All or wellnigh all of these many kinds were known to Aristotle. He described their form and their habits, their anatomy and development, all with such faithful accuracy that what we can add to-day seems of secondary importance. He begins with a methodical description of the general form, tells us of the body and fins, of the eight arms with their rows of suckers, of the abnormal position of the head. He points out the two long arms of sepia and of the calamaries, and their absence in the octopus; and he tells us, what was only confirmed of late,

that with these two long arms the creature clings to the rock and sways about like a ship at anchor. He describes the great eyes, the two big teeth forming the beak; he dissects the whole structure of the gut, with its long gullet, its round crop, its stomach and the little coiled coecal diverticulum: dissecting not only one but several species, and noting differences that were not observed again till Cuvier re-dissected them. He describes the funnel and its relation to the mantle-sac, and the ink bag which he shows to be largest in sepia of all others. And here, by the way, he seems to make one of those apparent errors which, as it happens, turn out to be justified: for he tells us that in octopus, unlike the rest, the funnel is on the upper side; the fact being that when the creature lies prone upon the ground with all its arms outspread, the funnel-tube (instead of being flattened out beneath the creature's prostrate body) is long enough to protrude upwards between arms and head, and to appear on one side or other thereof, in a position apparently the reverse of its natural one. He describes the character of the cuttle-bone in sepia, and of the horny pen which takes its place in the various calamaries, and notes the lack of any similar structure in octopus. He dissects in both sexes the reproductive organs, noting without exception all their essential and complicated parts; he had figured these in his lost volume of anatomical diagrams. He describes the various kinds of eggs, and, with still more surprising knowledge, shows us the little embryo cuttle-fish with its great yolk-sac, attached, in apparent contrast to the chick's, to the little creature's developing head.

But there is one other remarkable feature that he knew ages before it was rediscovered, almost in our own time. In certain male cuttle-fishes in the breeding season, one of the arms develops in a curious fashion into a long coiled whip-lash and in the act of breeding may then be transferred to the mantle-cavity of the female. Cuvier himself knew nothing of the nature or the function of this separated arm, and indeed, if I am not mistaken, it was he who mistook it for a parasitic worm. But Aristotle tells us of its use and its temporary development, and of its structure in detail, and his description tallies closely with the accounts of the most recent writers.[7]

Aristotle's account of the crustacea is equally brilliant: *cancer cursor* with its large gill-chamber; the minute description of the feet and claws of the crawfish, male and female; the beady eyes, moving either way; the notice of the third maxillipeds and the exopodites of the lobster; the careful description of the intake and discharge of water in all crustaceans; and so on.

We need not follow through the rest of the book, which deals with interesting but miscellaneous material on the sounds emitted by animals. Aristotle knows that the cause of the humming noise of some insects is the rapid movement of the wings; he knows that the grasshopper produces its peculiar sound by rubbing its legs, though he does not have the full details of this last performance. He knows also of fish, which squeak through stridulation, as he says of the gills, though really of the gill-covers, and of the true "voice" of the mammalian dolphin. And he distinguishes the different calls of birds in, for example, courtship and aggression. Impressive is his treatment of speech in man as part of the same pattern of behavior as that of other animals. The book concludes with observations on sleep and sex among various animals.

II *Reproduction in Animals*

With the fifth book we turn to the theme of reproduction, and this occupies three books, though, it seems, with a certain amount of interpolation. We are promised a systematic treatment: testacea, crustacea, cephalopods, insects, viviparous fishes, oviparous fishes, birds, and finally animals with feet, oviparous and viviparous, man being the only viviparous biped. It is hard to know what to single out in this wealth of information. Of course there is error; how should there not be? But even the error is often a false interpretation of a careful observation.

Aristotle's work on insects, apart from a curious indifference to butterflies, is exceedingly good. He knows about the emergence of gnats from tiny red bloodworms (551b27); he has watched flies appearing from a dunghill (521a21) and has found the grubs of horseflies in decayed wood (552a29). He is excellent on the hunter-wasp or ichneumon, which kills its spider, takes the carcass home, and lays eggs in it (552b27). His extended account of bees reminds one of Vergil (553a16ff). Or again there is a marvelously detailed account of generation of birds from eggs, and it is thrilling to read of the heart appearing, like a speck of blood, in the white. There is a good account of the pigeon family (562b3) and a speculative but informed notice of the cuckoo (563b14).

With sea creatures, the treatment of *mustelus laevis* was the theme of an admiring monograph by Johannes Müller in 1840 (565b2).[8] There is an excellent account of the mammalian dolphin (566b16). In a highly misleading and tendentious consideration of the eel, there is evident knowledge of the larva, which it was the pride of the nineteenth century to rediscover (570a15). There is an excellent discussion of the migration of tunny (571a15). So to the account of man, which has suffered more interpolation than most. Still it is refreshing to see man treated in context as a natural phenomenon, The picture is in general that of the best contemporary medical science. There are occasional glimpses of ordinary society: recessive traits are illustrated by a woman at Elis who had an affair with a Negro with the result that the dark pigmentation passed not to her daughter but to her grandchild (586a2); and likeness of the offspring to the father, by a mare in Pharsalus nicknamed "The Honest Wife" (586a13).

III *Animal Diet, Habitat, and Disposition*

The general theme of the eighth book, diet and habitat, begins with a fascinating account of the continuity of life. This should be seen in the context of the views expressed in his psychology about the different stages of *psyche,* nutrition, sensation, and intellection, each lower stage being subsumed in the higher and each higher stage adumbrated in the lower. Nature, says Aristotle, passes gradually from the inanimate to the animate, and it is impossible to draw exact boundaries (588b4); one would almost think that he knew about viruses. Similarly in plants we can trace a gradual ascent toward the animal, and Aristotle has excellent examples of animals resembling vegetables, such as the razorshell, sea anemone, or sponge, to illustrate his point.

What follows ranges over habitat, diet, migration, hibernation and other seasonal changes, animal pathology, the effect of pregnancy on health, and much else. It is a strange amalgam. Not a little is false and even fantastic, as that man alone does not die when bitten by a mad dog, or that mice do not drink in the summer. There is much curious lore, as that the pig is the only animal known to be liable to measles. Aristotle's strength is in his insatiable appetite for information and the strong element of personal observation, wherever possible. His weakness, odd in a teleologist, lies in his failure to ask the question "Why?" For example, he tells us merely that there is a river in Cephalenia with cicadas on one bank and not on the other (605b27);[9] even the uncritical Pliny attributes this to the lack of trees on one bank. But there are remarkable firsthand observations, expecially of marine life, of the dolphins (which he evidently loved), of the behavior of a crawfish caught in the same net as an octopus, of the parrotwrasse (*Starus Cretensis*), which browses and grazes so that it seems to be chewing the cud, of the eel-fisheries, of the fish which hug the shore, of the regular routes of migrating tunny, of the swordfish and its parasites, of the nest-building of the wrasse. For the rest we may note the association of climate with characteristics of physique and disposition. This was one of the brilliant discoveries of the medical schools, and again we see how assocation with his medical father helped Aristotle to become a great scientist.

The last book (since the tenth is patently spurious and does not concern us) turns to elaborate the theme of disposition. Aristotle begins with some masculine generalizations about feminine nature: soft, mischievous, complex, impulsive, cunning, compassionate, emotional, jealous, querulous, quarrelsome, despondent, pessimistic, shameless, mendacious, deceptive, alert, shrinking; the female has a more retentive memory, is more difficult to rouse to action, and needs less food. He notes, however, that with the bear and leopard the female has the advantage in courage, and with the Spartan hound in cleverness. Aristotle was a typical male Hellene and regarded the male as perfection and completeness.

For the rest, the book is a vast congeries of notes, systematized but on the whole lacking any real principle of interpretation. The weakness is the pathetic fallacy (the interpretation of animal behavior in human terms), and this is combined with the lore of the village fable, such as is familiar from Aesop or the Ananse stories from West Africa or Uncle Remus. Aristotle in fact notes the comparison with human habits (612b18). Throughout the book one vividly senses Aristotle's mind, inquisitive and acquisitive of factual information. "A partially tame woodpecker was once noticed placing an almond in a hole in a piece of wood to steady it for pecking; at the third peck it split the nutshell and ate the kernel" (614b14). "A lion was once noticed preparing to attack a boar; the boar stiffened its bristles in defence, and the lion turned tail" (630a2). He knows of what we might almost call circus-elephants (630b18). There is much excellent observation of birds, though one realized how gravely Aristotle was handicapped by the absence of field glasses. There is a remarkable description of the catfish now known as *Parasiluris Aristotelis* (621a21); it was only rediscovered with the work of Agassiz in the nineteenth century. But the great triumph of the book is its record of observation of insects.[10] Curiously, there is no extended passage on the ant. But there is a long, careful, and fascinating account of the bee (623b3), and one of the best things of all is his notice of the large wasp, which he calls Anthrene, biting off the heads of flies and carrying away the carcass; this is presumably *Bembex rostrata* of which Fabre made such marvelous observations.[11]

Researches is in one sense not a systematic treatise, and certainly does not provide anything like a thorough classification. But Aristotle is a systematist, and his basic principles are morphological. His work is in a sense preclassificatory. He is assembling the data which may provide a basis for classification. He sees, rightly, a complex variety of patterns, and he rejects facile solutions.

IV *Movement*

Two short monographs follow, *On the Movement of Animals* and *On the Locomotion of Animals:* there is no good reason to doubt their authenticity. Although they contain much of interest they need not detain us long. They are marked by a strongly teleological approach. The former is more metaphysical. Aristotle reasserts the case for an Unmoved Mover; movement depends on rest; and he uses this as an explanation of joints, whereby a limb moves from an unmoved point. He has grasped the lever-and-fulcrum principle of the joint. Furthermore, there must outside the animal be an unmoved medium to allow movement. This leads to an extended discussion of the Prime Mover and a curious digression on the mathematics implied in the myth of Atlas. Movement is of various kinds, but primary movement is movement towards fulfillment; it is the cause of coming-into-being and passing-away. In all movements, except the movement of the whole universe, and one or two examples of secondary movement, movement originates in the *psyche*. Movement is the conclusion of a practical syllogism: from the premisses "Every man ought to walk"; "I am a man," the conclusion is the act of walking (701a12). There is an interesting sidelight on Greek life in Aristotle's comparison between the movement of an animal and that of a marionette or of a child's go-cart designed to move in a circle by having wheels of unequal size (701b2); animal movement is more complex but the principles are the same. Another important comparison, between the constitution of an animal and a city-state (703a30), is connected with Aristotle's concept of order (*taxis*). When an animal or a community is well ordered, there is no need for the central authority to be involved in every decision: Aristotle is interested in the effect of heat in producing change: he continually reverts to this without examining it systematically. He concludes the monograph with a useful distinction between voluntary movement, involuntary movement (such as the quicker beating of the heart or erection of the penis), and nonvoluntary movement (such as breathing, sleeping, waking).

On the Locomotion of Animals is more like a piece of modern science in that it is the record of observations and deductions from them. Aristotle has, and exposes, his presuppositions: "One of these is that nature produces nothing purposelessly; it always produces the best result out of the possibilities permitted by the essential nature of each kind of animal" (704b14). Again we have a sudden glimpse of Greek life when we are told that athletes jump farther with weights in their hands (705a16).[12] This is on the face of it surprising, though it is known to have been Greek practice. Experiment has shown it to be true. In 1854, J. Howard, using five-pound dumbbells and taking off from a board, made a long jump of 29 ft 7 in; in 1892, K. Darby, using eight pound weights, made a high jump of 6 ft 5 in, and in 1900, R. H. Baker made a high jump of 6 ft 8¼ in.

Aristotle is still absorbed by the need for a resistant medium and for mobile and immobile parts in the moving animal. He distinguishes six different dimensions of a living being—upper and lower, front and back, right and left, and has some acute observations of the latter distinction in animals, and some interesting generalizations about carrying things on the left shoulder, hopping on the left leg, and stepping off with the left foot; there seems no awareness of left-handedness.

Most of the rest of the book comprises careful accounts, based on firsthand observation, of the locomotion of different animals: snakes, eels, the mullets of Siphae, crawling children, flatfish and rays, birds and insects in flight, men walking, horses prancing, crabs moving obliquely, birds walking, webfooted birds swimming—to instance but a few. He is particularly interesting on the necessity of flexion for locomotion: different methods of flexion were examined in detail and illustrated by diagrams (712a1). He has watched carefully the use of fins in swimming and of the tail in flying. One curious generalization is that animals endowed with blood move at not more than four points (707a20; 709b23). Altogether this is a rewarding monograph and shows Aristotle at his best.

V *Characteristics Acording to Natural Function*

With *The Explanation of the Constituents of Animals*—better known as *The Parts of Animals,* but we do not normally call blood a "part"—we return to first principles, and the opening book is one of the most remarkable in all Aristotle. There are two ways of studying a subject, roughly what we might call the amateur and the professional, corresponding to the man of general culture and the scientist, the one wide-ranging with a good judgment of the work of others, the other an original investigator in a specialized field; the one knowing something about everything, the other everything about something. To understand a subject is to understand its causes. This is a more useful principle of investigation than the principle of necessity (irrefragable scientific law) used by some scientists, who fail to distinguish between the absolute necessity governing the ultimate constitution of the universe and the relative necessity applying to the works of men and of Nature. Of these causes the most important is the final cause. We cannot understand a house without knowing what it is for, and Aristotle insists that the same is true of the works of Nature. Bergson agreed: we cannot understand the eye without knowing what it is for.

When we turn to principles of analysis Aristotle repudiates the method of dichotomy practised by the Platonists, which leads to artificial and false divisions, and he insists instead on the principle of natural division along the lines of essential characteristics. Then follows a passage, which demands extended citation (644b23); it won the warm approbation of Boyle:

> Natural substances are of two kinds, one group ungenerated, imperishable, eternal, the other coming into being and passing away. The former are of divine value, but our opportunities to study them are slight, since altogether there is very little accessi-

ble to our senses to form the groundwork of our investigation into them and all that we yearn to know. We are better off for the knowledge of perishable objects like plants and animals; we live among them. Anyone who is prepared to make a little effort can learn a lot about each class of them. Each group has its own charm. We may not have much grasp of things eternal, but their supreme worth lends a delight to our knowledge of them, surpassing anything in our own world; so an accidental momentary glimpse of those we love gives more delight than the precise observation of many other things, however important. On the other hand we have a larger and wider knowledge of our world, which gives an advantage in scientific understanding. The fact that it is closer and more familiar is some compensation compared with theological contemplation. I have already given my views on the divine. It remains to speak of animal life, so far as possible omitting nothing, mean or exalted. There are animals which offer no visible attraction, but to the eye of science the Nature which formed them offers innumerable delights for those with an understanding of causes and a philosophical temperament. It would be ridiculous to enjoy looking at their representations in painting or sculpture with pleasure in the artist's skill and not to take greater pleasure looking at the actual works of Nature, with all our grasp of their underlying causes. So we must not be childish and gripe at the study of the meaner animals. In every product of nature there is something to arouse our wonder. There is a story of Heraclitus. Some visitors came to call on him, and found him warming himself at the kitchen-stove. They checked their step, but he said 'Come in; don't be frightened: there are gods here too.' In exactly the same way we ought to move on to the investigation of any and every sort of animal without reservation. In each we can see Nature and beauty.[13]

With the second book we turn to a closer look at the subject. It is important to remember that what interests Aristotle is not the enumeration of the constituents, but the explanation, the causes. Composition is of three kinds, which correspond approximately to our chemical, histological, and anatomical. The first is composition out of the elements (earth, air, fire, and water), or rather the "powers" (*dynameis*) (wet, dry, hot, cold, with such qualities as weight, lightness, solidity, looseness, roughness, smoothness). The second is composition of uniform parts (bone, flesh, etc.). The third is composition out of nonuniform parts (face, hand, etc.). The distinction is important: if you fragment a piece of flesh you find smaller pieces of flesh, but if you fragment a hand you do not find smaller hands. This distinction introduces the main bulk of the work. After a surprisingly short discussion of the part played by "hot, cold, dry and wet" in physiology, he passes to a still briefer account of the uniform parts, in which we may notice his assertion that of all the animals man has the largest brain in proportion to his size and still more his association of this with man's upright stance (653a27), his insistence that a bone is never to be considered in isolation, but always as part of a system (654a32), and his analysis of kinds of teeth in terms of usage, whether for mastication or fighting (655b9).

He now turns to the nonuniform parts, and, as he says, is virtually starting afresh (655b28). Three constituents are essential to all animals. One takes nourishment, one ejects the residues, and one is the source of the life-principle. Aristotle asserts that man is the only known animal with a share of the divine—or at least that he has a larger share than any other (656b8).

So we embark on the magisterial account which occupies the rest of the work. First comes the head—brain; ears; eyes (with some magnificent observations of birds); hair (man's hairy head is explained by the action of the fluid of the brain through the sutures, and by the need for protection—658b3); eyebrows and eyelashes (interpreted, to Bacon's[14] despair, teleologically, that is, as purposed for protection of the eyes); nostrils (with some sensible remarks on the elephant's trunk); lips (with the double function of protecting the teeth and facilitating speech: Aristotle admires Nature's economy); tongue; teeth (with an interesting digression on the tendency of the male to have more effective offensive and defensive organs than the female—661b28); mouth or beak; and horns. Next follows the neck—larynx, windpipe and epiglottis; the action of the last is excellently described (664b25).

The next theme is viscera, the internal parts of animals endowed with blood. Aristotle has observed that their size in proportion to the whole animal changes with growth, an observation not repeated till the time of Leonardo da Vinci. These comprise: heart; blood vessels (chiefly the "great blood-vessel," which is the name Aristotle gives to the venae cavae and the aorta; but he is aware of a complex system, which he compares to irrigation-channels in a garden); the lung (always singular in Aristotle, though of course he knows the double structure); liver; spleen;

bladder; kidneys (here there are a number of observations, which must have been well in advance of the a priori views of the day, but which occasion misleading conclusions); diaphragm; membranes; stomach and intestines; gallbladder (Aristotle rightly says that its presence is variable in mice, and the fact that he extends this to men strongly suggests that he has examined aborted embryos, since the gallbladder does not develop till the third month); omentum; mesentery.

Next Aristotle examines first the internal, then the external parts of animals without blood—insects, testacea, crustacea and cephalopods. Incidentally, in this section there is a passage clearly indicating that *Researches* and a lost treatise on *Dissections* were amply illustrated, that an illustrated copy was available in the Lyceum, and that students attending the lecture course on *The Explanation of the Constituents* were expected to do library work (680a1). Of the observations we may note especially the account of the ink-bag of the sepia (678b36) and of the ova of the sea-urchin, which Aristotle had studied on the island of Lesbos (680a4).

Finally, we return to the external parts of the animals endowed with blood, viviparous and oviparous. One sentence throws a flood of light on Aristotle's general approach: "The head exists principally for the sake of the brain" (686a6); there is the teleology combined with a cautiously scientific awareness of the dangers of oversimplification. The account of man is fascinating. Again we have the emphasis on the upright stance, which is entirely justified biologically, though Aristotle, while examining the biological implications, including the relative size of the human foot, ultimately takes a theological view: man's upright stance is the product of his divine nature.

There is an excellent section on the hand. Aristotle holds the view that the hand is the result rather than the cause of intelligence. Some thinkers, he says, regard man as ill-structured and defenseless. In fact the hand is a talon, a claw, a horn, a spear, a sword, any tool or weapon you like; it can be any of these last because it can grasp any of these (687b2). Function is always the basic principle of explanation; thus, nails are an excellent device, in humans a protective covering for the finger-tips, in other animals with additional practical uses (687b22). Man is, as always, seen in the context of other animals, unique but one of them. So we pass to a general account of sex organs, excretory organs, feet and hooves, and finally to the ovipara, reptilians, birds, and fishes.

Altogether it is a monumental work, sometimes tendentious, sometimes in error, though the very errors often represent a partial advance in knowledge. In 1882, William Ogle published his admirable English translation. Charles Darwin wrote to him, "From quotations which I had seen, I had a high notion of Aristotle's merits, but I had not the most remote notion what a wonderful man he was. Linnaeus and Cuvier have been my two gods, though in very different ways, but they were mere schoolboys to old Aristotle."[15]

VI "The Generation of Animals"

The final work of this great sequence is *The Generation of Animals*. G. H. Lewes, whose tendency to denigration we have noted, appraised this most warmly of all Aristotle's work. The subject is a complex one, much of it is unfamiliar terrain to nonspecialists, and it does not lend itself to ready summary: the account that follows is inescapably arbitrary and perfunctory.

In the introduction Aristotle reasserts that Nature works toward a goal or end (715b16); hence, he is concerned with explanations, which he analyses in his doctrine of the four causes—final, formal, material, and origin of movement. Distinction of sexes is not universal, but among animals the primary principles of generation are the male and the female; male is defined as an animal generating in another, female as an animal generating in itself (716a14). The visible distinction between male and female arises from their essential nature; secondary sex characteristics depend on this primary sex distinction, as castration suggests. How excited Aristotle would have been by the discovery of hormones and their action!

Aristotle retains the analysis of animals into those endowed with blood and those without blood. He examines the sex organs of the former, male and female,and in so doing introduces what is in fact a more valuable basis of classification, between the oviparous and viviparous. Next comes a brief preliminary discussion of generation in bloodless animals. An exciting passage (already noted in the citation from D'Arcy Thompson) refers to what is properly called the "hectocotylization of the dibranchiate cephalopods." The male octopus has one arm charged with spermatophores, which it uses to impregnate the female. Aristotle has observed the act; he rejects, on reasonable grounds, the popular view among fishermen (which is in fact correct), that it is a sex act (720b32). The section on insects contains much error: not merely spontaneous generation, but the suggestion that the female inserts an organ into the male from below (721a13). Still, as so often, error is based on observation, and the distinction between egg and larva is notable.

The second part of the book contains a generalized theory of sexual generation. Aristotle examines, and rejects, a Hippocratic theory, which corresponds to Darwin's hypothesis of pangenesis, namely that semen is drawn from the whole of the parent's body. In the course of the discussion there appears a surprisingly modern distinction between inherited and acquired characteristics (721b29), though Aristotle believes in exceptional instances of the inheritance of acquired characteristics, like Mrs. Harris's husband's brother who was "marked with a mad bull in Wellington boots upon his left arm on account of his precious mother havin' been worrited by one into a shoemaker's shop."[16] Aristotle is aware too, as we have seen, of recessive characteristics, which skip a generation; we have another glimpse of the miscegenation at Elis, and may wonder what a Negro was doing there (722a10).

Semen is defined in a sentence that unfortunately tails off into manuscript corruption: "The object of semen is to be by nature something of such a sort that from it as origin come into being those things which are framed in accordance with nature. . . ." (724a17): the English is clumsier than the Greek. Semen is what Aristotle calls a residue or superfluity, and none the worse for that. Menstrual flow is also the discharge of a residue, which corresponds in the female to the semen in the male. In this way Aristotle arrives at his conclusion that both partners share in the generative process, the male contributing the form, the female contributing the matter. Aristotle's view that the menstrual blood is the matter of the embryo was connected with his view of blood as nourishment and with a curious theory of *concoction* which runs through his work and which has to do with the transformation of nourishment through the body's vital heat. This theory was not refuted till the time of Harvey.

These preliminary considerations extend into the second book. The existence of the sexes may be explained in terms of the material cause, and this requires further elaboration. Or it may be explained in terms of the final cause, namely the perpetuation of the species. This general assertion leads to a more elaborate classification of the modes of generation, linked to a theory of the opposites, hot and cold, moist and dry. Animals that are hot and moist are viviparous; animals that are cold and moist are ovoviviparous; animals that are hot and dry are oviparous, producing perfect eggs (which do not increase in size after laying); animals that are cold and dry are oviparous, producing imperfect eggs (like those of fishes); animals that are very cold are larviparous (a larva being in Aristotle's view an inchoate egg). In the next discussion, which overcame even Lewes's prejudice against Aristotle, Aristotle presents the debate between preformation and epigenesis. Does the young animal exist complete in the germ, or (as Aristotle holds) are the parts added successively? It is no mere play on words to call this a seminal discussion. Physically, semen is foam, a combination of water and hot air (*pneuma*). It contains *psyche*, the life-principle or soul, potentially but not developed into actuality.

The remainder of the book deals with generation in animals endowed with blood and viviparous. Aristotle is interested in embryology, and has a term of his own, *kyema*, for the primary mixture of the male and female up to the point when it is born or hatched. He reiterates that the female provides the matter, the male the life-principle; concoction takes place in the act of sex union, and conception can take place without the female enjoying a satisfying sex experience. The heart is the first part of the embryo to become distinctly actualized. Nourishment is supplied to the embryo through the umbilicus, as to a plant through the roots. The steady process of growth is reversed in the decay of old age: Nature is like a there-and-back runner (741b22). Nature employs the presence and absence of heat in the process of change.

Aristotle has an abstract and complex discussion, in which he isolates the end for the sake of which things exist, of things that exist for the sake of the end, and things that are used as instruments in the process of improvement toward the end.

He then examines the formation of the several parts of the body. We may note especially his discussion of the eyelids, which are brought to completion late in the process: "Nature produces nothing superfluous or without a purpose; it is clear then that the moment of production will be neither too early nor too late, since there would be no purpose and the production would be superfluous" (744a37). Notable is the correct identification of the nutritive function of the umbilical cord (745b20).The book ends with a discussion of hybridization and sterility as exemplified by the mule.

Next come the animals endowed with blood, oviparous and producing "perfect" eggs, chiefly birds. Aristotle thinks that the yolk is nourishment and the white holds the power of generation; he is wrong, as Harvey showed, but not unreasonably wrong. Then come the *ovovivipara,* the selachian fishes, which are internally oviparous and externally viviparous. Then follow the remaining *ovipara,* which produce "imperfect" eggs. Aristotle disposes of a number of old wives' tales and popular fallacies about both birds and fishes. The systematic examination concludes with an examination of generation in bloodless animals.

Aristotle believes in spontaneous generation and tries to provide a coherent account of it. Bees puzzle him, as well they might. The Greeks called the queen a king; it is clear that to Aristotle the word may include male and female. In fact he regards the king-queen as a self-fertilizing hermaphrodite, existing specially for the purpose of procreation. There follows this magnificent passage: "This seems to be the method of generation among bees on the basis of reasoned argument and apparent fact. But the facts are not adequately ascertained. If they are so ascertained in the future, we must trust the evidence of the senses rather than abstract argument, and theories if and only if they accord with the evidence" (760b28). It would be hard to better this as an exposition of one aspect of the scientific attitude.

We pass to more general considerations about the origin of sex differences. Aristotle follows his normal practice of discussing earlier theories. He accuses some of his predecessors of "guessing the likely outcome on the basis of probability and prejudging the nature of the situation before they see it in actuality" (765a27). He accepts the view that sex is determined by the origin of the semen from right or left, and its relative heat, as a partial truth. He regards the male as a determinative principle, active where the female is passive, and responsible for the concoction of the blood. It follows that the heart, the seat of the nutritive part of the *psyche,* and of the vital heat, is also the seat of sex determination. When we read that there is more probability of male offspring being conceived when the wind is in the north, we realize that for all his scientific stature Aristotle was liable to the most extraordinary aberrations, and that there is little here of more than historical interest.

There is a discussion of the resemblance of children to their parents—and an amusing glimpse of ancient cartoonists (769b18). The discussion of monstrosities is of some importance. They are in some sense contrary to Nature, since it is natural for offspring to resemble their parents. But they cannot be contrary to universal Nature, only to the general action of Nature (770b10); they are, so to say, improbable but not impossible. They are contrary to a particular order or ordinance (*taxis*), but they are not random or arbitrary. Other points discussed include the different numbers of offspring produced by different animals; superfetation (resulting from a second fertilization during pregnancy); the state of the offspring at birth; tumors of the uterine wall; milk; and the different periods of gestation, which Aristotle links with the revolution of the heavenly bodies.

Finally, he turns to secondary sex characteristics, like the color of the eyes or pitch of the voice. These do not belong to the essential nature of the animal. The eye exists "for a certain purpose"; the same cannot be said *in the same way* of its blueness. This discussion ranges over color of eyes, keenness of eye, ear and nose, which Aristotle analyses into the ability to perceive at a distance, and the ability to perceive minutely, and which he attributes to moisture in the organ or to the concentration of the percepts through long channels; varieties of hair, which he attributes to the thickness of the skin and to the moisture reaching the hair, grayness in age being due to a deficiency of heat and to consequent putrefaction through heat in the environment; vocal pitch; and finally teeth.

So—for *Dissections* and a projected work *On Growth and Nutrition* have not survived—ends this remarkable succession of studies. Of course they contain errors, limitations of observational technique, an almost total absence of experiment, presuppositions as outmoded today as the aether of nineteenth-century physics, faulty generalization, and a priori thinking. Yet when all this is said, one does not know which is the more amazing—the sheer volume and detail of the observations, carried out by one man with no modern equipment, or those passages which suddenly flash across the page and illuminate the whole nature of the scientific experience. Perhaps the finest tribute to his scientific stature comes in the last sentences of Lewes's book: "His mighty and eminently *inquiring* intellect would have been the first to welcome and to extend the new discoveries. He would have sided with GALILEO and BACON against the Aristotelians." [17]

CHAPTER 6

Psychology

I *Theory of Psyche: Plato vs. Aristotle*

THE Greek word *psyche* is conventionally translated "soul," but its scope is different. It covers functions which we should be inclined to analyze into at least four: the vital principle, the stream of consciousness, the moral personality, and the intellect. Hence some of the fallacies we find in Plato's proof of the immortality of the *psyche* in *Phaedo.* It may be a contradiction to attribute death to the vital principle, but there is no inescapable contradiction in assuming that either the moral personality or the intellect perishes. Plato, as always, lies in Aristotle's background. From Plato, and from normal Greek usage, he had inherited the use of the simple term for a complex entity. But Plato's own theory of the *psyche* was neither simple nor constant. Plato accepted from Socrates the importance of the *psyche* as the moral personality, the part of man that really matters, and in *Phaedo* developed this under Pythagorean influence into a series of arguments in favor of the *psyche*'s immateriality and immortality, as we have seen. But whereas in *Phaedo* the individual soul is single and simple (and this is indeed part of the case for its immortality), in *The Republic* Plato argues on grounds of psychological observation for a tripartite *psyche,* since we can observe Reason in conflict with Desire, and Temper siding now with the one, now with the other; in *Phaedrus* he produces an image of the *psyche* as a chariot in which the charioteer Reason tries to control the more or less unruly horses Desire and Temper; in *The Republic* the analogy of political structure puts Reason and Temper more closely together and Desire apart. On top of this *Timaeus,* the richest and most obscure of the dialogues, treats *psyche* as a cosmic principle, linked with but differentiated from intellect, and antecedent to the physical body of the world. What was left over from forming the world-*psyche* went to make the *psyche* of individuals, each associated with a star, each in ceaseless activity; it is distinctly suggested that only the reasoning part of the *psyche* is immortal. Finally, we may notice that in the tenth book of *The Laws* (898d ff.) Plato examines the question how an immaterial *psyche* can move a material body.

It is characteristic of Aristotle to devote the first book of his treatise on the *psyche* largely to the views of his predecessors.[1] Knowledge is good in itself and better when its object is important. So that the study of the *psyche,* which is the fundamental principle of animal life, has much to commend it as contributing to our understanding of nature. From this assertion he goes on to procedural problems. The knowledge of a thing's essential being helps us understand its attributes; the knowledge of its attributes helps us define its essential being; a definition that offers no information about attributes is valueless. This last is directed against Plato. Aristotle now establishes a point of some importance. The affections of the *psyche,* such as anger, gentleness, fear, pity, courage, joy, love, hate, are principles embedded in matter (403a25). This assertion is basic to Aristotle's approach. Plato, like Descartes later, was an extreme dualist. Mind is mind, and body is body, and how the twain shall meet is either a mystery or an impossibility. This view has been summed up neatly in an epigram variously attributed to Thomas Hewett Key and Douglas Jerrold: "What is matter? Never mind. What is mind? No matter." Against this Aristotle is clearly from the first allied with Spinoza and those who hold that mind and body are aspects of the same substance and separable only in thought.

The discussion of the views of his predecessors follows, and from it some further matter of general importance emerges. Aristotle finds two points common to earlier views of the *psyche* and accepts both with qualifications. The animate differs from the inanimate in motion and in perception. Previous thinkers had argued that the *psyche* was the cause of motion and was therefore in motion itself. Aristotle accepts the first part of this and rejects the second; the *psyche* moves without being moved. Previous thinkers had claimed that the *psyche* perceives and knows, but, following the principle "Like perceives like," added that the *psyche* must be composed of the elements which it perceives; Plato had given the argument a fresh twist when he claimed that the *psyche* knows the eternal, immaterial forms and must therefore itself be eternal and immaterial (*Phaed.* 78bff.). Aristotle accepts perception and knowledge as functions of the *psyche*, but rejects the particular theory of perception, which the conclusion assumed.

Another question arises directly from Plato's view of the *psyche*. Do the several activities of the *psyche* each involve the whole *psyche*, or has each its seat in a different part of the *psyche*? (411-a26). Is life itself in a single part, more than one part or the whole? If the *psyche* is naturally divisible, what holds it together? Not the body; rather the *psyche* holds the body together. But if the unity of the *psyche* were due to some other force, that force would itself be *psyche*. It is better to attribute unity directly to the *psyche*. In this way Aristotle asserts unequivocally the unity that puzzled Plato. In fact Aristotle does sometimes speak of parts of the *psyche*, but he is using the word loosely, and the preferable term is "faculties." The *psyche* is for Aristotle a single entity, performing a variety of operations.

After these preliminaries Aristotle is ready to move to his own theory, which offers an important example of his fundamentally biological approach. He defines *psyche* as "the primary actuality of a natural body which potentially has life" (411a27), or again "the primary actuality of a natural body endowed with organs" (412b5). By actuality (*entelecheia*) he means the realization of its essential being; thus *psyche* in its simplest sense is the vital principle without which something capable of life remains dead. Primary actuality relates to the possession of a faculty, secondary to its use. Thus our faculty of knowledge is actualized in a primary sense even when we are asleep, in a secondary sense when we are exercising it. The *psyche* is as inseparable from the body as an imprint from the wax in which it is made. Aristotle clarifies this difficult definition by two further examples. If an ax were a natural body its *psyche* would be its capacity to chop; without this it would cease to be an ax; with this it is an ax even when it is not actually being used for chopping. Again, if the eye were a living creature its *psyche* would be sight; without sight it ceases to be an eye except equivocally, but with the power of sight it remains an eye when it is not actually seeing.

Such a definition might well seem abstract and requires to be filled out with concrete analysis. To this Aristotle now proceeds. We can trace four operations associated with life: intellectual activity, sensation, locomotion, and nutrition. Aristotle does not however use locomotion as a cardinal principle of analysis. Plants enjoy the faculty of nutrition; animals add sensation to nutrition; humans add intelligence to sensation and nutrition; all are forms of *psyche*. Aristotle's account of the increasing complexity of the activities of *psyche* is astonishingly close to a modern account of evolution from lower organisms to higher. Aristotle's theory was not of course evolutionary; he believed in the fixity of species. But it is not wholly fanciful to say that all the evolutionists had to do was to transform his ladder of nature into an escalator.

The details of his scheme are historically interesting, and some of his treatment is of permanent value, but much is inevitably linked to an inadequate physiology. The minimal type of *psyche* is the nutritive, or—more fully—the nutritive and generative. Here, even in the simplest form of living creature, we see a teleological drive to reproduction, a kind of *élan vital*. This leads Aristotle to a digression upon the relationship of *psyche* to body in terms of his analysis of the four causes. *Psyche* stands to body as form to matter: it is thus the formal cause. It is the efficient cause, being the origin of motion in animate bodies, whether that motion is locomotion or qualitative change. And it is the final cause; all natural bodies whether of plants or animals, are instruments of the *psyche*, means to the end, which is the *psyche*.

Animals add sensation to nutrition. Sensation consists in the assimilation of the sense organ to the object: the hand becomes hot, the eye absorbs color, and so on. To receive sensations the organ must be in a mean state. This is perhaps clearest over temperature; we do not perceive the temperature of an object whose temperature is the same as ours, only one which is hotter or colder. (424a9). Aristotle applies the same principle to other types of sensation. To perceive white or black the eyes must be neither but must be capable of being either. Furthermore, whereas nutrition is an absorption of matter, sensation is an absorption of form without matter (424a17); when we see a stone, it is the form, not the matter that we have (literally) in mind. To put it in other words, sensation involves—indeed, is—a change in the medium; this change must be of a certain intensity or it will not be perceived; it must be of a limited intensity or it will destroy the organ. Aristotle in this analysis takes what we would term the physical basis of sensation and makes of it sensation itself. It is just, however, to say that his total view of the *psyche* is more complex than this might suggest and does include the principle of consciousness.

The objects of perception fall into three classes (418a7). The first comprises objects peculiar to one single sense, as color to sight, sound to hearing, flavor to taste; here perception is infallible, though false inference may be made about the object to which the color, sound, or flavor pertains. The second class comprises "common sensibles," perceptible to more than one sense. Such are motion, rest, number, shape, size; these may, for example, be felt as well as seen. The third may be called the indirect object of perception. In the strict sense we may be perceiving a white shape, but in an incidental but real sense we are perceiving Diares's son.

We may pass briefly over Aristotle's treatment of the individual senses, sight, hearing, smell, taste, and touch. Not all animals possess all of these, though all possess touch. Sight makes clear a number of points. Perception of color requires a transparent medium—it is not possible to perceive the color of an object placed in direct contact with the eye—and light is required to make the potentially transparent actually transparent. Aristotle denies that light has velocity (418b20). Similarly, sound requires the medium of air. Aristotle shrewdly suggests that just as light is always being reflected, so sound is always being refracted, though we generally fail to catch the echo. Smell too requires the medium of air or water. Taste and touch, which seem to operate by direct contact, are in fact operating through the medium of flesh (423b26).

II "*Common Sensibility*"

Aristotle has a speculative allusion to a "common sensibility" (*koine aisthesis*) (542a27).[2] He makes it clear that he is not referring to a sixth sense: there is no such thing. The matter is controversial, but here and in passages in the minor treatises he refers in somewhat similar language to some problems unsolved by his general treatment of perception. Such are: (a) How do we perceive the common sensibles? (425a14). Here Aristotle uses the term "common sensibility"; (b) How do we discriminate between the objects of different senses? (426b12). Aristotle says explicitly that it is by perception. In his little work *On Perception* he uses a phrase about the faculty "perceptive of all things" in this context

(449a3); (c) How do we perceive that we are perceiving? (425a12). Aristotle's plunge into introspection is obscure, but he seems to be insisting that it is through our senses. In the treatise *On Sleep* (455a16) he speaks in this connection of a "common faculty" (*koine dynamis*); (d) How do we account for the simultaneous inactivity of all the senses in sleep? This is expounded in the same passage from *On Sleep*. In it he refers to the heart as "a single controlling organ of perception" (455a21; cf. *Juv.* 469a13). To these questions some have wrongly added, (e) How do we perceive the incidental sensibles? (425a24). This is a real problem, and Aristotle does not offer a clear solution; what he does make clear is that the solution to this problem and the solution to that of the common sensibles are independent. But the first four points do cohere. It does not seem that Aristotle essayed a systematic solution, and it is wrong to think of "common sensibility" as a carefully articulated technical term, still more wrong to identify it with the heart. But with each of these questions Aristotle is groping toward an answer in terms of a power common to all the senses.

Associated with sensation and closely interrelated are the faculties of appetency, imagination, and locomotion. Aristotle's discussion of these is not wholly systematic. Appetency accompanies sensation, since sensation is accompanied by pleasure and pain, and with them comes the appetite for that which is pleasant. All animals have the sense of touch, and therefore appetency; hunger and thirst are elementary and obvious forms of this (414a32). Imagination (*phantasia*: the English word is not wholly satisfactory as a translation) is distinct from perception and from thought; from perception, because, though perception is presupposed, we can form images with our eyes shut, and because, unlike perception, it is fallible; from thought, because some non-rational animals have it, and it does not require ratiocination. Aristotle invokes imagination for four purposes: (a) the interpretation of sensation; it is probably here that he would place the perception of the incidental sensibles, though he does not follow this out; (b) the persistence of images in the *psyche* when the object is no longer directly perceived; (c) memory, which is impossible without images; and (d) dream-images. Locomotion is the subject of an appendix (432a15). Locomotion arises from appetency and imagination and is thus closely linked with the other two faculties. We can analyze the factors in animal locomotion into four: the object of desire, which moves without being moved; the faculty of appetency, which is moved and in turn causes movement; the animal, which is moved; and the bodily organ, which is the instrument of movement—and Aristotle characteristically breaks away from these abstractions into a fascinating aside on the design of the joints for producing motion by pulling and pushing.

III *Psyche and Reason*

The highest faculty of the *psyche* is reason. In his introductory remarks Aristotle says that there are obscurities about reason, but that it seems to be a distinct type of *psyche* and separable from the body (413b24). The obscurities intensify during his detailed treatment (429a10 ff). Thought bears the same relation to intelligible objects that perception bears to sensible objects. In an apparent contradiction he describes thought as a process of being acted upon by the object of thought, yet impassively. He must mean that though the intellect is receptive of intelligible forms, it is not altered or weakened by them in the way that sense perception may be destroyed when the object is too intense. It follows that the intellect is not fused with the body, but is separable from it. It must be remembered that the Greeks of Aristotle's day had not identified the brain as the seat of thought.

A number of questions now arise. The most important perhaps is what does Aristotle mean when he states that the intellect is capable of thinking itself (429b9).[3] (a) The Aristotelian commentator Alexander understood him in terms of the identity of the thinking mind and the object of thought. In thinking the intelligible form, the mind becomes the intelligible form, and in this sense it is the object of its own thought. (b) Zabarella took a subtler view. The identity of mind and object is a mental identity. In fact the mind knows its objects without self-consciousness. But this very fact means that as it reflects on its own operation it is aware of itself as distinct from its objects. (c) Aristotle may not be doing more than repeating the problem he has raised at the level of sensation and giving an unelaborated answer. (d) In *Metaphysics* the pure intelligence we call the Unmoved Mover "thinks itself." The theology there and here is very different, yet the phrases are strikingly similar, and Aristotle may be concerned to leave room for something of importance at the upper end of his system. (e) It has recently been cogently demonstrated that the phrase is Aristotle's way of expressing engagement in abstract thought.

Aristotle's psychology culminates in the distinction between passive and active reason, though the second term does not actually occur (430a10). There must be within the *psyche* a distinction corresponding to that between the material and efficient causes. Aristotle uses two analogies. An artistic or technological skill makes actual the potentiality of its material; the bronze is potentially a ring, but it requires the craft of the bronzesmith to actualize it. Again light turns colors which exist potentially into actual colors. In Aristotle's philosophy the actual is brought out of the potential by the actual. So the process of thought requires actual, active reason to produce the change in passive reason. This active intellect is separable, incapable of being acted upon, mixed with nothing, and in essence an actuality. It is continuously engaged in thought. But it is only when separated that it is its true self, and its true self is immortal and eternal.

Aristotle adds that we do not remember because active reason is impassible and passive reason destructible. The reference to memory is tantalizing, but it may be reasonably interpreted to mean that memory does not survive death. In other words, though a part of the *psyche*, the active reason is immortal. Aristotle has no doctrine of personal or individual immortality; in this he stands in stark contrast to Plato; but the acknowledgment of an immortal part in any form is due to Plato. The section ends with ambiguous words, which probably mean either "Without active reason, passive reason cannot think," or "Without active reason, nothing thinks" (430a25). Alexander and Zabarella identified active reason with God; it is described as "separable," which they take to mean "separated." But the distinctions between active and passive reason lie within the *psyche* (430a13), and the fact that active reason is its true self only when separated implies that it is not always so (430a22).[4] The God of *Metaphysics* is transcendent, active reason is immanent; the God of *Metaphysics* knows only himself, active reason has all knowledge and imparts it to us. It is possible, as Werner Jaeger argued, that the third book *On the Psyche* is early, written before Aristotle had formulated his later theology. Otherwise we must think of active reason as occupying a high, but not the highest place in the hierarchy of being.

IV "Monographs on Physiology"

Alongside this major treatise stands a series of minor works, already alluded to, called, without overmuch authority, *Parva naturalia* or *Monographs on Physiology.*[5] Their interest today is mainly historical. The first and most elaborate of the monographs is entitled *On Perception and the Objects of Perception;* its Latin title is *De sensu.* Living creatures must enjoy the faculty of perception or sensation, and of the senses Aristotle singles out sight and hearing as the most important. After the usual criticism of his predecessors, all of whom (he says, but immediately contradicts himself) make the organ of sight consist of fire ("Like to like"), he discusses the possible relation of each of the senses to a specific element, sight to water, hearing to air, smell to fire, and touch (including taste) to earth (438b17).

One of the most interesting passages in the monograph relates to color. From a later passage (442a20) we learn that his spectrum consisted of white, (yellow, a variant of white), crimson, purple, green, blue, (gray, a variant of black), black; he appears to admit yellow in its own right to make a total of seven; others are blends of these. But colors have as their basis white and black, and he suggests three ways in which new colors may arise: (a) from the juxtaposition of strips of white and black in different proportions, an impressionist technique, (b) from superposition (and Aristotle does here appeal to the technique of artists), and (c) from what we can only call chemical fusion, the explanation he favors himself.

Omitting hearing (because of its treatment in the work *On the Psyche*) he passes to smell and taste, which he regards as closely similar. Other animals surpass us in the sense of smell as we surpass them in the sense of touch and taste (441a1). Flavor and color are analogous, and Aristotle produces a corresponding spectrum of flavors: sweet, (smooth, a variant of sweet), harsh, pungent, astringent, acid, (saline, a variant of bitter), bitter. All are ultimately a mixture of sweet and bitter. Odor too is analogous to flavor and subject to exactly the same range of variety. Man has a peculiar sense of smell, which gives him aesthetic pleasure and is beneficial to his health (the odor bringing warmth to the chilly regions of the brain). Aristotle is curious as to how smell is possible for animals without lungs: he supposes that breathing opens a valve through which the odor penetrates, and other animals have no valve (444b23). But he will not admit that smell has any nutritive function.

The last sections are more general. Aristotle asks whether the objects of perception are infinitely divisible. He has proved in the treatise *On Movement* (the second part of *Physics:* book 6) that continuity implies infinite divisibility and assumes this. Every magnitude, however small, must be perceptible: a perceptible body cannot consist of imperceptible parts (445b14). A second question is whether it is possible to perceive two things simultaneously. Aristotle argues that we cannot perceive simultaneously two objects of a single sense, or two objects of different senses, and he rejects the view that there is an imperceptibly small time-lag between the perceptions. Aristotle's answer, indicated earlier, is that the central unifying faculty of perception enables us to do what the individual senses cannot of themselves do.

V "On Memory"

The monograph *On Memory* is in many ways the most interesting. Aristotle points out that memory and recollection are different: people with slow minds often have retentive memories, whereas those with quick minds are better at recollection. Memory is of the past, perception of the present, hope of the future; memory implies the passage of time. Memory involves imagination (*phantasia*), since it is concerned with mental pictures; Aristotle takes the metaphor of the impression of a seal on wax (we say "I have an impression that . . .") from Plato.[6] To contemplate such an impression or mental picture is like contemplating a painted portrait or (as we should say) photograph. This is a classical exposition of the theory of memory as representation, and it raises all the attendant philosophical problems. Recollection implies memory and results in memory; it applies where there has not been continuous awareness of the object or event, which has to be recovered. The method of recollection is by a process of association, and Aristotle, again starting from Plato,[7] formulates the laws of association, through similarity, contrariety, or connection (451b20). Many living creatures possess memory, but recollection, which involves reason, is peculiar to man (453a5).

VI *Sleep and Dreams*

There follows a series of monographs on sleep and dreams. The first is entitled *On Sleep and Waking.* Sleeping and waking are complementary; they are contrary states of the same part of the living creature. They involve both body and *psyche.* Living creatures that possess only the faculty of nutrition without sensation, i.e., plants, do not sleep. Sleep is the inactivity of all the senses. But this can occur in fainting or through pressure on the veins of the neck; sleep therefore is an affection not of the individual senses but of the central faculty of perception. The final cause of sleep is the protection of the living creature, since it requires rest to pursue its ends of perception and intellectual activity in wakefulness. The efficient cause is the heart or the corresponding region in bloodless creatures; Aristotle's physiology is based on the concepts of vital breath and vital heat, associated with the heart and the region around the heart.[8] The material cause is food, which by its inherent warmth produces rising vapor; awakening takes place when digestion is complete. The formal cause appears in the final definition of sleep—"a paralysis of the primary faculty of perception resulting in its incapacitation, taking place of necessity with the object of protection, since rest is a form of protection" (458a28).

On Dreams. Dreaming is not perception (since the senses are withdrawn); nor is it mere opinion (since we attribute perceptible qualities to dream-objects). Dreaming is something that happens to the faculty of perception, as sleep is, and it is connected with imagination. Sense perception can produce effects, which last beyond the original impulse: when we turn from sunlight to darkness the effect of the sunlight does not immediately pass from us: Aristotle uses some familiar optical illusions. He digresses to suggest further that vision is not merely affected by the object, but also affects the object, and produces with full credulity an old wives' tale that when menstruous women look at a mirror they see a cloud of blood.[9] Scientifically sounder is the demonstration of illusion through "Aristotle's experiment": if we feel an object (e.g., a marble) between crossed fingers, it seems to be not one but two (460b20). Aristotle's explanation of dreams, then, is that the objects of sense remain perceptible after the departure of the external object, and in sleep they have little to compete with them. True perception can take place in sleep, as when a sleeper answers a question or is dimly aware of hounds baying, but the awareness is dim, and these are not dreams, any more than the real thoughts which occur in sleep (e.g., "This is a dream"). The mental image derived from the movement of the senses when they are in a state of sleep, insofar as they are asleep—that is a dream (462a30).

On Prophecy in Sleep is a brief appendix. Aristotle's approach is rational and eschews dogmatism, whether credulous or skeptical. If a dream is fulfilled in an event it must be a cause, sign, or coincidence (462b27). Aristotle notes that some dreams are distortions of events: a slight warmth may occasion a dream of a furnace. Some dreams however provide an impulse to action and are thus causes. Aristotle's explanation is rational; some action is on your mind, you dream of it, and the dream reinforces your will to act. Others are simple coincidences. Often dreams have no results. Prophetic dreams are not sent by some god: volatile people have such a fertile imagination that sometimes their visions must come true. People with unstable minds also do not let their own intelligence dominate them and are more open to outside impressions. But that people dream of their friends is readily explicable in that their minds tend to dwell on them. The skillful interpreter of dreams is thus the man with an eye for likenesses. One feels that Aristotle would have been fascinated by the work of the Society for Psychical Research, by the investigation of mediumistic personalities, by Soal and Rhine's work on ESP and precognition, and by the theories of J. W. Dunne and their dramatic expression by J. B. Priestley.[10]

VII *Birth and Life*

The remaining monographs are biological, but it is convenient to treat them here. *On Length and Shortness of Life* is tied to an outdated physiology. Aristotle thinks in terms of the elements and their qualities, hot and cold, dry and moist; it is interesting that these "opposites" were singled out by the medical schools.[11] The living creature is naturally moist and warm, and adequate moisture and warmth are the secret of longevity. Excess of sexual emission, overwork, a cold climate, and shortage of nourishment all shorten life, as they dry or chill the creature. Trees are long-lived, because their moisture, being viscous, is not easily frozen or dried up, and because they are always renewing themselves. The male tends to be longer-lived than the female, because his upper parts, where the warmth resides, are larger than the lower. There is not much here to attract Dr. Comfort's attention.

The final monograph, known in Latin as *De Juventute,* should be entitled something like *On Youth, Old Age, Life, Death, and Breathing;* the last section is sometimes wrongly treated as a separate work. The seat of life is the heart, and by the heart the *psyche* is set on fire (469b16). But fire can be put out by dying out and by being extinguished; these correspond to death by old age and death by violence. There is a sense in which we must bank our fire to keep it going. This leads Aristotle to the topic of breathing. All animals with a lung breathe (he uses the singular, as elsewhere, treating the lungs as a single entity). After introducing the subject, he in his usual manner presents and criticizes the views of his predecessors before presenting his own. The life and state of the *psyche* depend on heat. That heat may be destroyed by cold, but equally it may burn itself out. Breathing introduces a gentle coolness, which has the effect of banking the fire. Later he adds that fish achieve the same effect through water but are suffocated in air (479b8).

After elaborately examining the anatomy and physiology of various kinds of animal, Aristotle gives an excellent summary of his conclusions: "Birth is the first participation in nutritive *psyche,* taking place in warmth. Life is the continuation of this. Youth is the growth of the primary organ of cooling, old age its decay, the prime of life the period in between. Death by violence is the extinction or weakening of the heart; for destruction may occur by both means. Natural death is the weakening of the same part through the passage of time to an appropriate end; among plants this is known as withering, among animals as death. Death in old age is the weakening of this part because old age prevents it from keeping cool. So much for the definition of birth, life and death, and explanation of their occurrence among living creatures." (479a29 ff).

VIII *Summary*

Aristotle's psychology, out-of-date in some ways, dogmatic in others, retains its interest. In the first place, Aristotle, unlike Plato, approaches psychology as a naturalist. This attitude lends wings to his incidental observations; it also endows his whole procedure with general soundness. When he is wrong he is still along the right lines. This impression is intensified by the monographs. Secondly, Aristotle's comprehensive treatment is itself impressive; he has the breadth of vision to bring together the life of plants, animals, and men on a single canvas. Thirdly, the analytic devices that form a part of his general philosophy were seldom used to better effect. The distinction between form and matter, themselves correlatives, is admirably applied to the relationship of *psyche* and body. The four causes are effectively employed as an instrument of analysis. Fourthly, he is aware, as earlier thinkers were not, of the complexity in the term *psyche,* and by separating the different levels and faculties of *psyche,* he went far in eliminating the ambiguities involved. Finally, he does not let his primary concern for natural science deter him from the consideration of things which cannot be weighed and measured, nor does he allow metaphysical presuppositions to impose upon his scientific procedures.

CHAPTER 7

Metaphysics

WHAT we call metaphysics Aristotle called "first philosophy." The title *Metaphysics* means simply the lectures, which followed the course on "physics"; in this sense it would be better rendered something like *Advanced "Physics."* As we have it the work comprises fourteen books. The great German scholar Werner Jaeger dissected these and drew conclusions about the composition of the several parts;[1] with the swing of the pendulum the critic is himself being criticized. Certainty is not possible. But Hesychius's catalog of Aristotle's writings speaks of ten books on *Metaphysics*. This is likely to be ours with the omission of II, which was inserted after the Greek numbering was complete, and had to be given a small letter (A = I, B would normally be II; this is inserted as α), and which is by a minor Aristotelian named Pasicles; V, which is a collection of definitions and appears independently in Hesychius; XI, which falls into two parts, one of which was expanded into III-IV, VI, and the other consists of some student's notes on *Physics;* and XII, which seems to be an independent treatise on the First Cause. It looks as if V and XII were written fairly early, though XII was much revised to reach its present form. Aristotle's earliest course of advanced lectures may have been something like I, the first part of XI, XIII, XIV. But he later revised and expanded this into the ten books which Hesychius knew, and later still it took the form we know. We shall here ignore books II and XI, as being either not Aristotle's work or covered elsewhere, and treat the rest in the most convenient order.

I *Argument Against Plato's Forms*

"All men have a natural aspiration towards knowledge" (980a22). So Aristotle begins, and shows, as in *Posterior Analytics* (99b32) how we advance from sense-perception to memory, so to experience, and to scientific expertise, which understands causes as well as facts. Wisdom consists in the knowledge of first principles and primary causes. To be wise a man must have a grasp of universal principles; he must be able to master difficult subjects; he must be precise, and clear in exposition of causality; and he must pursue knowledge for its own sake, not for utilitarian ends. Wisdom (which he equates with first philosophy) is a theoretical science, concerned with teleology, independent, divine; here, in the full sense, is a liberal study.

It is, as we have noticed, characteristic of Aristotle to begin with a survey of his predecessors, and thus what follows is a document of rare importance for the history of early Greek thought. But Aristotle is not compiling a history; he left that to his successor, Theophrastus. Aristotle is asking his own questions, and he views his predecessors in the light of those questions. In this sense he imposes his own outline on them, and gives a misleading picture. Cherniss in a monumental study concludes that in treating Presocratic theories Aristotle "has not only perverted details but has also obliterated the problems these theories had to meet and obscured the relationship of the doctrines to one another." [2] The judgment, magisterial and provocative, has received wide acceptance; yet it seems unduly unsympathetic. Aristotle was no fool, and he possessed the full text, whereas we grope through fragments.

He starts his survey from the four causes he established in *Physics*—the being, essence, or form; the substrate or matter; the origin of motion; and the purpose, good, or end. In the light of these he examines earlier thinkers. He suggests that most of the original philosophers were looking for the material cause, the substrate out of which the world emerged and into which it would be resolved. He is not wrong in this, though we would add that they were intensely interested in the process of change, and that he ignores Anaximander, who does not fit into his scheme. The earliest thinkers were monists; they looked for a single principle—water, air, or fire. Then came pluralists, first Empedocles, then Anaxagoras, and finally the Atomists. The first clear statement of an efficient cause is found in Anaxagoras who, taking Mind as the cause of order and arrangement, stood out like a sober man among babblers. Earlier writers, the poet Hesiod, the philosophic poet Parmenides (who stands somewhat apart from other thinkers), and Empedocles (who behind his obscure language takes Love as cause of good and Strife of evil) seemed to speak of Love as a cosmic motive force. Formal principles were recognized by the "so-called" Pythagoreans (perhaps Aristotle thought of Pythagoras as legendary), who were fascinated by number, and used numbers analogically to explain such things as justice, intellect or opportunity, and indeed the system of the universe in general and in detail. Finally, in Plato the material cause is the "Great and Small," the formal cause the Forms, and ultimately the One. None of Aristotle's predecessors, he claims, has really identified a final cause, though it is embryonically found in Anaxagoras, Empedocles, and Plato.

The most important remaining part is his criticism of Plato's Theory of Forms, since there is a sense in which the rejection of this theory is the starting point of his own system. In Plato's system material objects are manifold, changeable and unreal. But to any group of things called by a common name there is a corresponding Form, single, eternal, real, unchanging, and perceived by the intellect alone. Against this scheme Aristotle brings a number of arguments to bear: (a) The Forms merely land you with two lots of things to explain instead of one; this is unfair and untrue; (b) If a common name implies a Form, there must be forms of negations—not merely injustice but "non-horse"—and of extinct beings (like the dodo—and why not?), and of relations; (c) Plato argued that to explain the similarity between two men, there must be a "third man," the Form of Man, in which both share. But what of an individual man and the Form of Man? Do they too not require a third man—and so *ad infinitum?* (d) The Platonists had come to identify Forms with numbers; Aristotle reasonably says that the Form of Man may be a formula, but it is not a number; (e) Plato never really explained the relation between Forms and particulars; in *Phaedo* he was content to say: "By Beauty beautiful things are beautiful;" [3] Aristotle shows that the Forms are not the material cause; they are not the efficient cause of motion or change; they are not the purpose; they are not even the formal causes, for, being transcendent they contribute neither to the being of material things nor the knowledge of them. (To Plato only the Forms can be known.)[4] Aristotle dismisses Plato's language about "patterns" or "participation" as empty language and poetic metaphor (991a21). The simple fact is that Aristotle, the scientist, believes in the reality of the material world; Plato does not.

II *On Definitions*

It will be convenient next to look at the definitions Aristotle gives in book V, since that stands apart from the others.

BEGINNING (or "principle"): the first point from which a thing exists, comes into being or is known.

CAUSE: (a) the inherent material, e.g., the bronze (or metal) of a statue; (b) the form, pattern or definition of the essence, e.g., 2:1 (or number) of an octave; (c) the origin of change or rest, e.g., the father of a child; (d) the end or goal, e.g., health as the aim of exercise.

ELEMENT: primary component.

NATURE: primarily the being of those things which contain in themselves as themselves a source of motion.

NECESSARY: primarily the simple which cannot be otherwise; also used of things which are necessitated by something else.

ONE: primarily used to describe a substance; a kind of starting point of number; but loosely and variously used.

BEING: in an absolute sense, of any of the categories; relatively, of accidental attributes.

SUBSTANCE (the conventional rendering, but the Greek word is the abstract noun from "to be"): (a) the ultimate substratum, which cannot be further predicated of anything else; (b) a "this" with individual and separate existence.

SAME and OTHER: these may refer to accidental or essential similarities or differences. They play a major part in Plato's later metaphysics, but Aristotle treats them cursorily.

OPPOSITE: used variously of contradictories, contraries, relative terms, privation and possession, extremes, incompatibles.

PRIOR and POSTERIOR: in space, time, motion, potentiality or arrangement; in knowledge (noting that a thing may be logically prior, but perceived later); in nature and substance.

POTENTIALITY (the word also means power): basically the power to produce or experience change.

QUANTITY (how large): that which is divisible into constituent parts.

QUALITY (of what kind): primarily the differentia of the substance, e.g., two-footed of man, four-footed of horse.

RELATIVE (in relation to something): (a) numerical, (b) as active to passive (here Aristotle does use the actualizing of the potential, e.g., something which produces heat is relative to something being heated), (c) as subject to object.

COMPLETE (or perfect: the Greek contains the root of "goal" or "end"): (a) a single thing such that it is not possible to find even one of its parts outside it, (b) that which cannot be surpassed in excellence, (c) that which has attained its end, a worthwhile end.

LIMIT: (a) furthest point, (b) form of a spatial magnitude, (c) end, (d) substance or essence. "The beginning is a kind of limit, but not every limit is a beginning."

THAT IN VIRTUE OF WHICH: form or essence; matter or substrate; and in general of the causes.

DISPOSITION: order, physical or logical.

STATE: a disposition in virtue of which a thing is disposed well or badly, e.g., health.

AFFECT: a quality in virtue of which alteration is possible; the alteration itself. The Greek word also means suffering or disaster.

PRIVATION: strictly, the non-possession of an attribute which a thing of its genus would naturally possess.

TO POSSESS (have or hold): to control; to be receptive of; to contain.

TO COME FROM SOMETHING: principally in relation to (a) matter, e.g., the statue comes from bronze, (b) cause of movement, e.g., the fight came from an insult, (c) the compound of matter and form, e.g., the line comes from *The Iliad*, (d) a part of a form, e.g., man comes from two-footed.

PART: that into which a quantum can in any way be divided.

WHOLE: (a) that which does not lack any of the parts of which it is said to be a natural whole, (b) that which contains its contents in such a way that they form a unity.

MUTILATED: used of a whole which has lost a significant part but retains its essence.

GENUS: that which underlies the differentiae.

FALSE: (a) things which cannot be substantiated, (b) statements of the nonexistent, (c) people who make such statements.

ACCIDENT: (a) that which applies to something and is truly

asserted, but is not necessary or usual, e.g., finding a treasure may be an accident of gardening, (b) that which applies to a thing in virtue of itself, but does not belong to its essence.

III *Aporematic Teaching*

We now return to the main course of lectures. At the outset of Book III Aristotle lays down a program of problems, which he elaborates in the remainder of the book. So far his course has consisted of a critical survey of cosmological theory in the light of his doctrine of four causes. He takes off from this point:

(a) Are several sciences concerned with the investigation of the causes, or one only?
(b) Is that science concerned solely with the first principles of substance or also with the axioms which are the starting point of scientific demonstration?
(c) If it is concerned with substance, do all substances come under one science or do they require several?
(d) Are all substances perceptible through the senses, or are there others? (He has in mind Plato's Theory of Forms, and a refinement by which mathematical objects occupied an intermediate status between the full forms and the material world.)
(e) Is the investigation concerned strictly with substances, or with their attributes as well?
(f) Are the first principles the classes or genera under which the substance falls or are they its component parts?
(g) If the genera, are they the proximate or ultimate genera, e.g., man or animal?
(h) Is there any cause besides matter? If so, is it separable from the material object? Is there one or more than one? Is there in fact anything apart from the concrete object? (Again he has Plato in mind.)
(i) Are the first principles limited qualitatively or quantitatively?
(j) Are the first principles of perishable things themselves perishable?
(k) Are unity and being essentially the same, the substance of all that exists? (So the Pythagoreans and Plato.) Aristotle calls this the knottiest problem of all.
(l) Are the first principles universal, or are they like particulars?
(m) Do they exist potentially or actually?
(n) Are numbers, lines, figures, and points in any sense substances? No book shows more clearly Aristotle's ability as a teacher. He begins by asking questions. He proceeds to show the

difficulties raised by each of the questions. For the time being the student is left to work out his own solutions. The treatment is, in the technical term, aporematic. Ross well says that *Metaphysics* "expresses not a dogmatic system but the adventures of a mind in its search for truth." [5] Further, the apparent preoccupation with Platonic views is no mere relic of Aristotle's own past. It is an existential attempt to grapple with almost the only systematic attack on these problems current in the Athens of his day.

IV *Law of Contradictions*

With the fourth book he begins his answers, and in the words "'Being' is used in several senses" cuts away years of sophistry (1003a33): he will return to this (VII 1028a10). There is a science, which Aristotle calls "first philosophy" and we, because of this work, call "metaphysics," which studies being as being. Although "being" is variously used, it is always used of substance and its modifications. Being and unity, though not identical in definition, are closely associated, and to study being is to study unity; further, to study unity is to study plurality, which is the absence or privation of unity. Thus in a sense all is grist to the philosopher's mill, since he is concerned with being and its modifications; he deals with the first principles. But the philosopher's field of knowledge must also extend to what the mathematicians call axioms, since these are at the basis of the search for truth. Aristotle takes as the most certain of all principles the law of contradiction: "the same attribute cannot at the same time and in the same respect both belong and not belong to the same subject" (1005b19). He feels so strongly on the importance of establishing this that he offers a series of proofs of its validity: for example, if all contradictory statements are true of the same subject at the same time, then all things will be one; the blunt fact is that all men do make some unqualified judgments, and Aristotle is content to stick to the common sense of that. He is guarding against the epistemological nihilism of the great agnostic Protagoras. Aristotle denies that one opinion is as good as another, or that there is truth in appearances; even Protagoras's fellow-townsman Democritus saw through that. Those who deny the law of contradiction need to be convinced that there is an unchanging reality, something which is prior to sensation. But Aristotle is wise enough to see that cogent proof of ultimates is not possible; the starting point of a demonstration cannot be demonstrated (1011a13). All we can ultimately say in defense of the law is that the alternative is a thoroughgoing relativism, which Aristotle regards as absurd. He then asserts the second of the so-called "laws of thought," the law of the excluded middle: "there cannot be an intermediate between contrary statements, but we must either affirm or deny any single predicate of any single subject" (1011b23). We do well to reject those who make logically contradictory statements, such as "Everything both is and is not." We do well also to reject those who make any form of sweeping generalization, such as "Everything is" "Everything is not" "Everything is at rest" "Everything is in motion." These and similar statements are oversimplifications and false.

V *Book VI: Being as Substance and Essence*

Book VI is brief but basic. It begins with a distinction between various branches of knowledge. Particular sciences treat some particular aspect of being, but do not discuss its fundamentals. Intellectual disciplines may be practical, productive or theoretical. Natural philosophy belongs to the last group; it deals with objects capable of movement, and for the most part with substance considered as bound up with matter. (Aristotle takes his favorite example: "snub" implies matter because only a nose can be snub; "concave" does not.) Mathematics is a theoretical science, but whether its objects are separable from matter is not clear to Aristotle; it must be remembered that to the ancients geometry (=land-measurement) and astronomy were branches of mathematics. First philosophy is distinguished from natural philosophy because its objects are separable and immutable. No true science can deal with the accidental; scientific knowledge deals with what is always or generally true. But there are accidental causes; otherwise we should be under the sway of determinism.

Aristotle is at last ready to get down to fundamentals and repeats his statement that "Being" is used in several senses. It may indicate what a thing is, a *this*, a concrete object; or its quality, quantity, etc., but the first is clearly primary, the substance, primary logically, epistemologically, and chronologically. But what is substance? It belongs to natural bodies and their parts. It is used in four major senses: the essence (Aristotle has a curious phrase which we so render: literally "the what-it-was-for-a-thing-to-be"); the universal; the genus; the substrate. The substrate is "that of which the rest are predicated, whereas it is not predicated of anything else" (1028b36). What then is the substrate? In one sense, matter (in a statue the bronze); in another, shape (the pattern of its form); in another, the combination of the two (the finished statue). The third is clearly not primary. Most obviously matter would seem to be the substrate; strip away everything else, and matter remains. And then Aristotle's residual Platonism asserts itself. Against the logic of his argument he rejects matter. Substance must be separable and individual; it must be form.

He goes on to discuss essence. The essence of anything is simply what it is. Essence belongs only to species of a genus; in the primary sense only substances have essence, and therefore only substances have definition. From this he passes to essential complexes, such as his favorite *snub nose, odd number, female animal, equal quantity* where the adjective cannot be explained apart from the noun; he does not allow such compounds to have essence or definition in the strict sense. Definition is by genus and species, and these can be defined only by enunciation of characteristics. Then are things the same as their essences? Yes, provided that we eliminate accidental predication.

"Some things which are generated are generated naturally, some artificially, some spontaneously, all by some agent, out of something, so as to come to be something" (1032a12). They come to be one of the categories; they are generated out of matter; the agent in natural generation is the so-called "formal nature," which has the same form as the thing generated. Aristotle's example is one he uses repeatedly: "man begets man." His discussion of artificial generation is less clear. Take a bronze ring; the matter is bronze, the form is annular and this shape is the proximate genus; but a bronze ring has matter in its formula. Though it emerges out of the matter in one sense, in another it emerges out of the absence of form, the privation. This curious concept recurs from time to time; we have met it in his book of definitions. Privation characterizes matter; it is form, but negative form, the absence of appropriate form.[6] For Aristotle to treat it as a positive factor is a fanciful aberration. What is generated is not form or matter, but an individual object which combines the two. Form is not generated; essence is not generated. A bronze sphere is generated; not bronze or sphere. Further, if form existed apart from individual things, there would be no generation of individual things. This hits at the Platonists: Aristotle means that if forms are substances, individual substances cannot be generated from them, for one substance cannot contain another. In an individual human we have a general form in particular flesh and bones, the same form in different matter. Matter is thus the principle of individuation and plurality (1034a5).

Essence has been equated to definition, and this raises a number of questions. Should the definition of a whole include the definition of its parts? Should it include matter? Is it possible to define a concrete whole, which embraces matter and form, i.e., sensible objects? When we talk of an individual man we mean a concrete whole compounded of this particular formula or definition and this particular matter treated as a universal. There is thus no definition of the individual since individuals are distinguished by matter which is strictly unknowable; our apprehension of them is direct through perception or intuitive reason. Definition belongs to the universal, the form; a ring may be of bronze or stone or wood; the matter does not pertain to its essential substance; strip away the material and the circularity remains. (But is this valid? For (a) strip away the circularity and the material remains: this is Aristotle's earlier problem about the substrate; (b) if Aristotle is really concerned about individual objects—a *this*—the bronze is an essential part of *this* ring compared with other rings.) Aristotle is uneasy; he then suggests that perhaps matter should not be altogether eliminated, but this is mainly because of his difficulty in conceiving a disembodied man, and he does not present a completely consistent picture.

Toward the end of Book VII he returns to substance, and now shows that substance is not to be equated with the universal, since substance pertains to individuals and universals are common: this argument is turned against the Platonic Forms. Substance is of two kinds: the concrete thing and the formula or definition (i.e., the formula combined with matter, and taken generally). Substance is a principle and a cause (1041a10). It is meaningless to ask why a thing is itself; the only real why is "Why is X predicated of Y?" ("Why is so-and-so cultured?" etc.) In this we are seeking the cause, or, in philosophic terms, the essence. The question can be rephrased. "Why is the matter what it is?" ("Why are those materials a house?") We are seeking the cause in virtue of which the matter is some definite thing. This is the form; and the form is the substance of the thing.

VI *Matter and Form*

Much of Book VIII is recapitulatory, and if Aristotle thought his students needed to recapitulate, we may do the same. Substances include natural elements, living beings and their parts, the cosmos and its parts. Some thinkers add the Forms and the objects of mathematics. Substance is used of the essence and the substrate; it is more appropriate to genus than to species and to universal than to particulars. Further, since essence is substance, and definition is the verbal expression of essence, to study substance is to study definition and essential predication. Substrate is substance: in one sense matter (dynamically defined as that which is a "this" not actually but potentially); in another the formula or shape; in another the combination of the two.

Matter is clearly substance (Aristotle is not always so clear about it); it is that which undergoes the process of change; but it is potential substance (e.g., building materials). Form is also substance (e.g., a receptacle for possessions and living beings); it is actuality. The combination gives the concrete house. Aristotle's doctrine of matter and form is important to grasp: (a) matter is potentiality, form is actuality, (b) matter is always the matter, the potentiality, of a definite thing; the bitter is the proximate matter of bile, not of mucus; bronze is the proximate matter of a statue, not of a human being, (c) hence, matter and form are not separate but relative to one another, (d) matter is the potentiality to be or not to be: the bronze may not become the statue, (e) matter is the principle of individuation, (f) matter as such is unknowable.

VII *Potentiality and Actuality*

Aristotle passes from the static analysis of reality in terms of matter and form, which occupies Book VIII, to the dynamic analysis in terms of potentiality and actuality, which occupies Book IX. Potentiality, like being, has many senses. An important sense is the possibility of being affected; another is the potentiality of acting. Potentiality may be properly applied to rational and nonrational beings. Some potentialities are innate; others (e.g., playing a musical instrument) are acquired by practice (an odd statement: perhaps he means that one is not even potentially a flautist before starting to practise); others depend on performance (again, one is not even potentially a builder before starting to build).

Actuality Aristotle defines, not very clearly, as "the presence of the thing—in a different sense from potential presence" (1048a31). Mere motion is not of itself an actualization, because it is incomplete, a process (e.g., slimming, learning, walking, building). Now just as matter is the matter of a particular thing, so potentiality is the potentiality of a particular thing, e.g., not merely is semen not the potentiality of a statue, but earth is not the potentiality of a statue; earth is the potentiality of bronze, and bronze is the potentiality of a statue. Everything is thus form or actuality with reference to something "below" it and matter or potentiality with reference to something "above" it. There is a great ladder of being, with (as Aristotle makes clear elsewhere) God, who is pure form, pure actuality, at the top, and (as we may logically suppose, seeing that it is not directly knowable) pure matter, pure potentiality, at the foot. The dynamic analysis adds one other vital point to the static. Actuality is prior to potentiality (1049b4), prior logically (it is because it can be actualized that the potential is potential), chronologically (man is generated by man; the actual is produced out of the potential by the actual; Aristotle's answer to the children's riddle is that without question the chicken came before the egg), and substantially (because everything which is generated moves towards its end as a principle; the act of building is to be seen in the thing being built). Aristotle concludes, a shade irrelevantly, with a discussion of being in the sense of truth, and not-being in the sense of falsity.

It would be hard to overestimate the importance of this dynamic analysis. It was no doubt suggested to him by adumbrations in Plato. In *The Republic* Plato had stated that light creates in the eye the possibility of seeing, and in objects the possibility of being seen,[7] and the faculty of sight is in fact a favorite illustration with Aristotle (e.g., 1050a24). Furthermore, in *Theaetetus* Plato had tried to explain how we may possess a piece of knowledge without grasping it. But he had not systematized his insights; it took Aristotle's particular genius to do that. One of the great stumbling blocks of ancient thought had been dropped by Parmenides. Parmenides had argued that change is logically impossible. For if a thing is to change, we must say that it *is not* today what it was yesterday or that it *was not* yesterday what it is today; yet how can we say of anything which is, that it is not? Aristotle's answer was formulated in the twelfth book (1069b19): "everything comes into being out of that which is, but out of that which is potentially, not actually."

VIII *Contrariety*

The tenth book is probably the most neglected portion of *Metaphysics*, and it is indeed less original and exciting than what has gone before. It starts from a discussion of unity: "*one* has four basic usages: the naturally continuous, the whole, the individual, and the universal." But these diverse uses do not give a definition. It would seem that oneness is essentially indivisibility; it is thus the starting point of measurement. Unity is not a substance but a predicate, which has in some sense the same meaning as "being." Aristotle then discusses briefly the related concepts of identity and similarity, and the opposite concepts of plurality with otherness and dissimilarity. He gives a more detailed treatment of contrariety, which is maximum difference, and shows that there is only one contrary for any one thing; he distinguishes contrariety alike from contradiction, privation, and relativity. Intermediates stand between contraries, belong to the same genus, and are a blend of contraries. Aristotle means that gray and (apparently in his view) red are blended of black and white, which he regards as the contrary extremes of color, whereas there can be no intermediate between shape and color. Next he takes otherness of species, which goes with identity of genus, and shows why male and female and white and black are not specific differences; this is a fascinating glimpse of a biologist exploring his subject. The book ends with the contrariety of "perishable" and "imperishable" and a hit at the Platonists.

IX *Nature of Mathematical Objects*

The last two books of the ten-book course are also somewhat neglected, and we may partially follow that neglect, since their interest is mainly historical. Forming a treatise on the nature of mathematical objects, they lead to an extended criticism of Platonic number-theory. Aristotle starts from the question whether there is some immutable and eternal substance besides sensible substances. Claims have been made for mathematical objects and Platonic Forms and sometimes (certainly by Speusippus and possibly by Plato himself) the two have been equated. Aristotle claims first that it is impossible for the objects of mathematics to be in sensible things, since two solids cannot occupy the same space, and since on this theory all the other potentialities and characteristics would be immanent, not transcendent. The second point seems ill-conceived: the attack on Platonism distorts his objectivity. Further, if the ultimate mathematical unit of the point is indivisible, the sensible object would also be indivisible. But mathematical objects are not separable either. (a) We would be involved in a mathematical solid, itself composed of planes; they would require hypermathematical planes to explain them; these would require superhypermathematical lines, and so ultrasuperhypermathematical points. (b) Abstract mathematics cannot solve concrete problems. (c) Some mathematical propositions do not involve the Form of Triangle (e.g., the congruence of two triangles: there is only one Form). (d) Spatial magnitudes must be prior to theoretical magnitudes (Aristotle's emphasis on solid earthy reality comes out). (e) Mathematical magnitudes detached from spatial extension have no obvious cohesion. (f) In abstract mathematics the solid is generated from point, line, and plane; but the solid whole is in nature prior. (g) Body is a kind of substance; points, lines, and planes are not. It follows that mathematical objects have at best a relative existence. There is no such thing as female or male apart from living creatures, but there are attributes peculiar to an animal, as female or male. There are no such things as mathematical objects apart from sensible things, but there are attributes peculiar to sensible things, as line or plane. Aristotle commends mathematics for its beauty; the thought is curiously close to that of G. H. Hardy in *A Mathematician's Apology*. "The principal aspects of beauty are order, proportion and definition—all strongly evidenced in the mathematical sciences" (1078a37).

Aristotle now reexamines the Theory of Forms, pointing to its genesis in Heraclitus's view that the sensible world is in a state of flux, and Socrates's search for definitions in ethics. This is the famous passage where Socrates's contribution to philosophy is summed up as "inductive reasoning and general definition"

(1078b28), and he is explicitly said not to have treated universals as separate. This is the clearest evidence that Plato puts his own theories into the mouth of Socrates. Aristotle's rejection of the Theory of Forms is repeated from Book I, with slight additions.

He next treats the view that numbers are substances, and first causes of existing things, criticizing the views of Pythagoras, Plato, Speusippus, and Xenocrates. His argument turns on the addibility of numbers. If all units are addible, then number remains mathematical and cannot have anything to do with the substance of things. If units are inaddible then there cannot be a Form of 2 or of 3; it is in fact impossible to generate numbers. Idle to go on: if his criticisms seem strained, the theories he is criticizing were fantastic.

In the last book he returns to the attack on new grounds. All thinkers take contraries as their first principle; but contraries are predicated of a subject and cannot be first principles. Platonists take the Great and the Small, or the Many and the Few, or that which exceeds and that which is exceeded—or they add Unity, treating that as Form and the other two as matter; their statements are badly expressed. But unity implies a substrate; it is predicated of something else and has no substantial existence; so too the equal, or the great and the small, are predicates, not substances. Further, an eternal substance cannot be compounded of elements. The Platonists went wrong further in using an out-of-date formulation in terms of Being and Not-being, and mistreating these terms. Aristotle repeats his contention that the presupposition of existence is not non-existence but potential existence. He rejects the identification of Forms with numbers and repeats some of the criticisms of the previous book. To take the Good as first principle is more reasonable, but not to identify it with unity. Further, if unity is good, it follows that plurality is bad; it follows also that the Bad is the potentially Good. Aristotle is not commending this interesting thought but treating it as absurd. The Platonists err in his view in making every principle an element, in making contraries principles, in making unity a principle, and in making numbers primary substances, separable entities and Forms.

Aristotle now turns to Speusippus, though he does not name him (1092a12). Numbers cannot be the causes of things in any of the Aristotelian senses of cause. Aristotle's argument is not wholly persuasive, but his position is sensible. Number is plainly not the efficient or the final cause. To a Greek accepting the elements, earth, air, fire and water, it might make sense to say flesh was formally (or materially?) three parts fire and two parts earth, but fire and earth are at least as important as three and two. Further, if number is of the essence of things, then numerical coincidence ought to mean identity; yet there are (in Greek) seven vowels, seven strings to the scale, seven Pleiades, seven years before most animals use their teeth, and seven heroes in the legendary attack on Thebes. Identity? We may legitimately see certain analogies between numbers and things: no more. We must stress that Aristotle's preoccupation with the Platonists is no mere relic of his own past. Platonism was a live option—in some sense (apart from atomism) the only alternative live option. A work like W. K. C. Guthrie's *History of Greek Philosophy* spends considerable time discussing recent theories about the philosophers he treats. We need not be surprised if Aristotle treats his subject matter similarly.

X *Eternal Substance*

All this seems slight indeed by comparison with Book XII. This has been rightly seen as the coping-stone of *Metaphysics*.[8] Aristotle has used the term Theology for the study of objects which are separate and immutable; it is the primary science; it is, at the last, his First Philosophy (cf. VI 1026a16). Book XII is a systematic study of theology, and stands, as we have said, on its own. The subject of his enquiry is substance. There are three kinds of substance: sensible and perishable (e.g., plants and animals), sensible and eternal (Aristotle has in mind the heavenly bodies), and immutable. Sensible substance is open to change; this implies a substrate in which the change takes place, matter. Change is of four kinds, of substance (coming to be or passing away), of quality (alteration), of quantity (increase or decrease), of place (locomotion). For change to take place there must be form, privation of form, and matter (which is relative to form). In change something (matter) changes into something (form) through the agency of something. But proximate matter and form do not "come into being." Substance may refer to matter, form, or combination in the individual. Different things have different first principles—obviously—but the pattern is consistent: a pattern of actuality and potentiality (corresponding to form and matter). The cause of a man is: (a) his elements: fire and earth as matter, and his specific form, (b) some external cause, as his father, (c) the sun and its oblique course. (These are secondary moving causes: Aristotle believes that the proximity of the sun in summer aids generation.)

So far this has been, so to speak, revision. We now come to the core of the book. Substances are the primary reality; if they are all perishable everything is doomed to destruction. But there are two imperishable entities, motion and time. If time were generated there must have been no time before; but that very "before" implies time; and motion and time hang together. The only continuous motion is locomotion; the only continuous locomotion is circular. There must therefore be an eternal circular motion. To produce this there must be an eternal substance, capable of causing motion (unlike Plato's Forms), whose very being is actuality, and thus immaterial. (It might seem that potentiality should precede actuality, but Aristotle reaffirms that this is not so.) In fact there is something which is moved with an unceasing circular motion—the outermost layer of the sky. There must therefore be beyond it an eternal unmoved Mover, who is substance and actuality. Aristotle, forgetting that he has dismissed Plato's explanations as empty metaphors, says that this causes movement in the way that the object of love moves the lover (1072b3); we may, if we will, think of Beatrice and Dante. The Mover is the final cause of the universe; he is also the efficient cause, but only as he is the final cause. Aristotle does not here state where he is to be found: elsewhere he varies between placing him on the outside of the universe (*Phys.* 267b6) and declaring that he is not in space at all (*Cael.* 279a18). The first Mover must enjoy bliss. Being immaterial his activity must be intellectual, and the object of his thought (as Aristotle elaborates after a digression) must be the best possible. "Therefore Mind thinks itself, since that is the best possible object, and its thinking is a thinking upon thinking" (1074b34).[9]

It has recently been shown that this does not give us a God engaged in self-contemplation, but it is Aristotle's way of saying that God is engaged in abstract thought. We thus have a picture of the Unmoved Mover as the eternal unmoving cause of motion, pure actuality containing no matter, living in blissful abstract contemplation transcendent and without knowledge of the world he moves, and Aristotle applies to the Mover the name God. "We affirm then that God is a living creature, eternal, the highest point of goodness; continuous and eternal life and duration pertain to God; for this is what God is" (1072b29).

This then is Aristotle's theology. His God is not in any real sense a Creator; he is certainly not Providence; he has no awareness of evil, no interest in the world, no love for man; and it remains one of the paradoxes of history that the immeasurably subtle medieval scholastics found it possible to identify this *dieu fainéant* with the everworking Father proclaimed by Jesus, whose very name is Love, and who is there, caring, if even a sparrow falls to the ground. Aristotle's God rather points forward precisely to the gods of Epicurus, who borrowed his theology from Aristotle without acknowledgment, and later to the Deists of the seventeenth and eighteenth century. Only at one point does he seem to involve God in the universe. He allows that the supreme good exists separate from the universe, but is also to be seen in the orderly arrangement of its parts, as the order of an army depends upon its own standard of good and (or, possibly, i.e.) its commander (1075a14: a much-mistranslated sentence).[10] This is another poetic metaphor and hardly to be pressed, though it is enough to show that Aristotle is uneasy about the logic which has excluded God from the world.

The digression just mentioned is a late insertion; it is also an aberration. Aristotle suggests that the motion of the heavenly bodies requires a plurality of unmoved movers and goes to the theories of Eudoxus and Callippus to depict a whole nest of concentric spheres. As for Aristotle motion is imparted to the outermost sphere and communicated to the whole, each of these further spheres must have a second sphere, equally transparent, rotating in the opposite direction, to counteract the effect of its motion. This gives him fifty-five spheres, something as follows:

	Deferent spheres		Reacting spheres
Saturn and Jupiter	2 × 4 = 8		2 × 3 = 6
Mars, Mercury, Venus	3 × 5 = 15		3 × 4 = 12
Sun	5 = 5		4 = 4
Moon	5 = 5		0 = 0
	33	+	22 = 55

Aristotle was not an astronomer; he was in error even by his own principles in not assigning reacting spheres to the moon. If we accept Eudoxus's figure of three spheres for Sun and Moon, this, says Aristotle, would give forty-seven; he has forgotten that he has not assigned reacting spheres to the moon! This lands him with fifty-five, or forty-seven, more Unmoved Movers. Then he becomes impatient, as may we, with these calculations, and asserts roundly that there can be only one heaven or universe (1074a32). At the end of the book, for his last word, he quotes Homer:

> The rule of many is not good: let there be one ruler.[11]

CHAPTER 8

Ethics and Politics

IN the body of writings which have come to us under Aristotle's name several cover the broad field of ethics. Of these the work known as *Magna Moralia* was probably written by an Aristotelian scholar in the century after Aristotle's death,[1] and the slighter work *On Virtues and Vices* is a later syncretistic work. The other two, *Ethics according to Eudemus* and *Ethics according to Nicomachus,* both authentically represent Aristotle's thought, as manifested at different stages of his career, and recorded or edited by different students. Nicomachus's version is fuller and more mature, and we may legitimately concentrate on it as representing Aristotle's best thought. But man for Aristotle is always man in society, and ethical problems are not to be divorced from social problems. The last words of *Ethics* lead straight into a new course of lectures on *Politics.* These were certainly authentic, though the work as it stands is a slightly miscellaneous amalgam. Two other works in the field of political and social science survive. *The Constitution of Athens* is one of a series of 158 monographs on the constitutions of Greek states compiled under Aristotle's direction; it bears his imprint, though he perhaps did not write it himself. The three-volume *Domestic Economy* is, however, undoubtedly later and not authentic.

I Ethics

Ethics is the most immediately rewarding of Aristotle's surviving works. It is more readable; it is packed with vivid and diverting character-sketches. Aristotle was a scientist, and in order to analyze human behavior, he had to collect a gallery of portraits of men in action. The subject matter and method of analysis seem familiar to us; he is dealing with a world we know; social patterns may change, but, as Goethe once put it, "Mankind advances, but man remains the same." *Ethics* is arguably still the best book to place in the hands of anyone who wishes to wrestle with ethical problems. The acceptable answers (whatever they may be) may not be present, but the pertinent questions assuredly are. Henry Jackson once called it "an *aperient* book."[2]

Ethics for Aristotle is the attempt to find the ultimate meaning or purpose of human life. He plunges straight in. "Every science and every subject, every action and every choice appears to aim at some good; so the Good has been well defined as the object at which all things aim" (1094a1). Plainly there is a wide variety of limited targets, but at the last we must suppose either an infinite regress or an ultimate good, and this is a matter of the highest practical importance. The science that studies this goal is readily identified as political science, but this is not an exact science, and it is not for the immature. The goal itself is readily named as Happiness (the Greek word, *eudaimonia*, has overtones of "blessedness" on one side and "success" on the other); the problem is to define Happiness.[3]

Here Aristotle lays down a cardinal principle in opposition to his master Plato: "*We* must begin from what we know" (1095b6). Most people pursue Pleasure, but that is to put humans on a level with domestic animals. Honor is better, but it leaves us dependent on the approbation of others; and even Excellence (*arete*) may be coupled with inactivity or actual misery, while Wealth is a means not an end. Aristotle touches on his own solution—Contemplation—but defers his treatment to the end of the whole work. He proceeds instead to reinforce his rejection of Plato's position. Plato centered his scheme on the Form of the Good, a concept so ultimate that it was "beyond reality." Aristotle with sturdy common sense asks what is the use of that to a weaver, carpenter, or doctor faced with pressing practical problems. Plato's Form of the Good, detached and absolute, is not practicable or attainable by man (1096b33). The real Supreme Good is always an end and never a means; it is self-sufficient; and it pertains to man in society. To find it we must examine the "function" of man; Aristotle's view is of course teleological. This is "an activity of the *psyche* in a manner conforming with or at least not opposed to reason" (1098a7); the good man will perform this with excellence. And it is a lifetime job: "One swallow does not make a spring."

It will be noticed that Aristotle is not identifying a precondition of happiness, but happiness in itself; this is not far from Spinoza's

"Blessedness is not the reward of virtue, but virtue itself." Aristotle goes on to stress that excellence must be displayed in activity. About the part which prosperity contributes to happiness he is less clear; it seems to be a normal precondition, but nobility of character shines through adversity (1100b30). Happiness then consists in activity carried out at a perfect pitch of excellence, with an adequate endowment of worldly goods. But what is this excellence? It belongs to the *psyche;* it is rational and spiritual. We may in fact begin to translate it as "virtue," noting a distinction between intellectual virtues such as wisdom and moral virtues such as liberality and self-discipline.

II *Virtue Defined*

In the second book then he concentrates on virtue and eventually arrives at his famous definition (1106b36): "Virtue is a fixed disposition involving choice; it consists in a mean relative to us, which is rationally determined, that is, as an intelligent man would determine it." Again we are impressed by Aristotle's sturdy common sense. Virtue is a disposition; the exact Latin translation of the Greek word gives us "habit." Despite the "situation ethics" supporters with their capacity for recording or constructing exceptional situations, we do not take a fresh decision with every action we make;[4] I do not ask myself of every woman I meet, "Shall I commit adultery?" or of every statement I make, "Shall I tell a lie?" We acquire certain dispositions or habits. But these arise out of a deliberate choice we have made in the past, and they direct our choices for the future.

This is clear. What then did Aristotle intend by the doctrine of the mean? At this point in lecturing it seems that he would display a diagram (1107a33) showing the field of activity in the first column and the virtue between its corresponding vices in the other columns. Exact translation is at times difficult, but the diagram went something as follows:

FEARS AND THEIR ABSENCE	Rashness—COURAGE—Cowardice
PLEASURES AND PAINS	Profligacy—SELF-DISCIPLINE—Insensibility
GIVING AND GETTING MONEY	Prodigality—LIBERALITY—Lack of liberality

(on a larger scale)	Vulgarity—MAGNIFICENCE—Meanness
HONOR AND DISHONOR	Vanity—NOBILITY—Ignobility
(on a smaller scale)	Ambition—AMBITION—Lack of ambition
ANGER	Hot temper—GOOD TEMPER—Indifference
SOCIAL INTERCOURSE: TRUTH	Boastfulness—TRUTHFULNESS—False Modesty
:ENTERTAINMENT	Buffoonery—WITTINESS—Clodhopperliness
:SOCIABILITY	Obsequiousness—FRIENDLINESS—Surliness
EMOTIONS	Shamelessness—MODESTY—Shamefacedness
ATTITUDE TO OTHERS' FORTUNES	Envy—RIGHTEOUS INDIGNATION—Malice

A number of points leap out from this analysis. The virtue stands at a mean point between two extremes, one of excess, one of defect. But it is not an arithmetical mean; courage is closer to rashness than to cowardice. What is more, right action looks like an extreme to those who are wrongly disposed: the brave man appears rash to the cowardly and cowardly to the rash. Further, Aristotle seems to suggest that the mean may vary with the individual and the particular circumstances; moral virtue in fact demands an activity at the right time, in the right conditions, towards the right people, for the right purpose, and in the right manner (1106b21). The doctrine of the mean is a convenient tool, and is not to be pressed beyond that. For example, there is no mean in adultery; it is not possible to commit adultery with the right woman, at the right time, and in the right manner (1107a16). Again, we must clearly state that virtue is in essence and definition a mean, but in value an extreme; here the modern analogy of a dartboard or target shows exactly what Aristotle intends, for the bull's-eye is in essence and definition a mean but in value an extreme. Aristotle's view may lead to a kind of middle-class morality—there are interesting parallels in Confucian China—but it is at least moral, and withal cool and sane.

III *Voluntary Action and Individual Virtues*

Before examining in detail the various virtues, Aristotle examines the concept of voluntary action. Praise and blame are bestowed on voluntary actions, pardon and pity on involuntary. An action is involuntary when performed under external compulsion or through ignorance, though some actions are properly called "mixed," like the jettisoning of cargo in a storm; in the abstract one would never perform it, yet under compulsion of external forces one might choose it (1110a8). This leads to a discussion of choice (*prohaeresis*), the term which has already appeared in the definition of virtue. This is a rational procedure and is thus narrower than voluntary action. Children and animals exercise voluntary action but not choice; spur-of-the-moment action is voluntary, but it is not governed by choice. Choice is not desire or passion (which the lower animals experience); it is not a wish (we can wish for impossibilities); it is not an opinion (which is judged factually not morally). Its object is not ends but means, and its instrument deliberation. Choice then is a deliberate reaching out for things within our power (1113a10). It would be hard to overestimate the importance of Aristotle's analysis here. It follows that virtue and vice are within our power. Aristotle rejects the Socratic paradox that "no man goes astray willingly;" indeed, throughout he is hard on Socrates, even putting his characteristic mock-modesty in the catalog of vices. We are responsible, ethically and before the law, not only for actions arising directly out of deliberate choice, but also for actions arising out of an ignorance we have culpably failed to dispel ("Ignorance of the law is no defence") or out of a disposition or character which is the result of our past choices.

This concludes the preliminaries, and Aristotle proceeds to a closer examination of individual virtues. We need not follow him in detail through this, though much of it is interesting and indeed entertaining. His method is completely different from that of Plato, who tended, following Socrates, to draw all the virtues together until they were almost synonymous. Aristotle draws them apart, limits and narrows them. His distinctions are careful, even minute. Thus he differentiates true moral courage from patriotic courage (inspired by patriotic emotionalism—or fear of punishment), courage born of experience (like that of the professional soldier), courage inspired by anger (and therefore irrational), courage proceeding from an inherent optimism, and courage proceeding from ignorance (1116a16 ff).

The crown of the virtues for Aristotle we have called nobility: it means literally "greatness of *psyche*" (*megalopsychia*),[5] and has been variously rendered by the translators; we have no precise English equivalent, the more so as it is not a quality which we today admire (1123a34 ff). The noble man is of course a good man; we cannot imagine him, when in military defeat, retreating so fast that he has to swing his arms to keep up the pace, or behaving dishonestly in any circumstances. He appears to us, bluntly, as a pompous ass. He prefers giving benefits to receiving them, because he does not like being in anyone's debt. He behaves haughtily to the upper classes, condescendingly to others. He is open in his likes and dislikes of people; more interested in truth than in reputation. He does not bear malice. He is no gossip; he does not speak ill of others except when he wants to be deliberately insulting. He prefers uselessly beautiful possessions to those that are useful or valuable. His movements are slow, his voice deep, his speech deliberate. Of course some of these are excellent qualities, but on the whole it reads like a caricature of a Victorian *paterfamilias*. It is no caricature, but the Victorians could enter into Aristotle's framework of thought better than we.

IV *Justice*

With the fifth book Aristotle takes up a new topic, justice or honesty. Renford Bambrough has called his discussion "a paradigm of philosophy," because "Philosophy consists in drawing the kinds of distinctions between concepts that Aristotle draws in this passage, and in marking the kinds of connections between concepts that Aristotle marks in this passage."[6] Bambrough compares him as a philosophical tightrope walker with Wittgenstein. Pamela Huby too compares his general methods with those of modern linguistic analysts: Aristotle takes an ethical term, studies the way it is used, classifies the usages, and suggests changes where these are imprecise.[7] What Aristotle does is to note that the word "justice" may be equivalent to moral virtue in general, or it may be a particular virtue operating in social relationships where gain and loss are involved. The man who is just in the first sense will inevitably be just in the second; the man who is just in the second will not necessarily be just in the first, for an honest businessman may well be a coward. Aristotle concentrates on the second sense, and again we note his rejection of Plato's synthetic treatment.

Particular justice is of two kinds, distributive and remedial. Distributive justice means the distribution of resources, whether in the family or a business enterprise or the state, in proportion to merit. We do not think of the state as distributing resources; on the contrary. But, as John Burnet put it, the Greek citizen regarded himself as a shareholder in the state rather than as a taxpayer; and perhaps his attitude was in the long run healthier.[8] Remedial justice is no respecter of persons; in that sense it does not operate in proportion to merit; it rights wrongs. The followers of Pythagoras tried to define justice as reciprocity. Aristotle rejects this as a general definition, leading him to identify a third kind of justice, commercial justice, or the exchange of services; it operates on the basis of proportion not of strict equality, and money is its convenient intermediary; the cobbler and builder do not exchange services directly, but the services of each are evaluated in terms of money.

Aristotle identifies just dealing, somewhat implausibly, as the mean between committing injustice and suffering injustice. He makes more useful distinctions, as between justice in the state and justice in the home, or between natural and conventional justice. This last is the origin of the later Stoic distinction between natural law and civil law, a distinction of vast importance since it enabled the modification of civil law in a more humane direction. In the final section Aristotle examines the inner springs of action, and makes the distinctions which correspond precisely to those between accidental death, manslaughter, justifiable homicide, and murder. He is doubtless, though he does not say so, following the practice of the law courts. His words have also affected legal practice, especially through his discussion of equity, "a rectification of law where it is defective because of its generality" (1137b27).

V *Intellectual Virtue*

Plato isolated four virtues which Ambrose later termed "cardinal"—courage, self-discipline, justice, and wisdom. Aristotle, who has Plato in mind even while he rejects his approach, has in fact treated the first three. He now turns from moral virtue to intellectual virtue. For if the mean we are to practise is rationally determined, moral virtue presupposes intellectual virtue. Within our intellect we can distinguish two faculties, one concerned with knowledge, and the other with deliberation, choice and so action; the first is theoretical, the second is practical, but both are concerned with truth. Five dispositions of our inner being may help us to this—intellectual cognition; technical expertise; practical good sense; rational intuition; and theoretical wisdom. The distinctions are admirably and skillfully drawn. Aristotle proceeds to an extended examination of practical good sense, which is roughly equivalent to political sense; it is the medieval *prudentia*, but by no means the modern English "prudence." [9] The man who has it deliberates well and takes the best practical decisions. He must be aware of both general principles and particular facts, and this in turn requires a certain degree of experience and maturity. Practical good sense is quite distinct from intellectual cognition and rational intuition, which do not deal with particular cases. It shows itself in deliberative excellence, which reaches right practical conclusions by sound reasoning, in common sense, and in good judgment. Practical good sense implies moral virtue; moral virtue implies practical good sense. But virtue is not (as Socrates thought) wholly intellectual, though the intellectual and moral virtues are closely related. Finally, practical good sense is inferior, subordinate, and subservient to theoretical wisdom.

VI *Continence and Incontinence*

The seventh book, with its treatment of internal conflict, has received much approbation in recent years. Aristotle makes a fresh start by distinguishing vice, incontinence, and bestiality, and their opposites, virtue, continence, and saintliness, but the interest is concentrated on the discussion of incontinence and continence, or weakness and strength of will.[10] Socrates claimed that all wrong action arises from ignorance. Aristotle, as might be expected, takes the commonsense view: we know what it is, with Ovid's Medea,[11] to see and approve the better course and follow the worse, or, with Paul, to fail to do the good we would, and do the evil we would not.[12] Aristotle rightly says that the state of mind involved should be closely examined. He begins by asking how the incontinent man may be said to know the good he rejects. It is simple, and true, to say that such a man has the knowledge potentially but not actually, because desire prevents the knowledge from becoming actual at the moment of choice. But there is more to it than that. In a practical syllogism (Aristotle does not use the phrase) the major premiss is a general statement, the minor deals with particular things, and the conclusion is an action.[13] If you have before you the major premiss, "Everything that is sweet is pleasant," and the minor one, "This is sweet," you will be led by desire to the practical conclusion of tasting it, even though you may be faced with another major premiss (to extend and make precise Aristotle's example), "Everything that contains sugar leads to an increase in weight," because, under the influence of desire, it is the minor premiss, "This is sweet," which determines your action, not the minor premiss, "This contains sugar." We may approximately say that to know, desire, and do the right is virtue, to know and do the right while desiring the wrong is continence, to know the right but to desire and do the wrong is incontinence, to be ignorant of the right and to desire and do the wrong is vice. Aristotle's analysis overemphasizes the role of reason, and does not really include man as a battleground of conflicting desires, but it is arguable that it required the advent of psychoanalysis to make any effective advance in our understanding of the problem.

VII *Pleasure*

Aristotle next turns to the topic of pleasure.[14] His treatment is curiously fragmentary. He has adverted to the subject once or twice. He takes it up briefly at the end of the seventh book, lays it aside, and takes it up again in the tenth. It will be convenient to examine the passages together. Plainly the study of pleasure and pain is within the province of the moral philosopher, since virtue and vice are exercised in the field of pleasure and pain (1152b5 cf 1104b4). Aristotle examines three views: first, the view of his contemporary Speusippus that pleasure is never a good thing, second, a view expressed in Plato's *Philebus* that some pleasures are good but most are bad, and third, also found in *Philebus*, that even if all pleasures are good, pleasure is not the supreme good.[15] He was of course a member of the Academy and shared in the discussions which led to the writing of *Philebus*. Commonsensical as always, Aristotle defends the view that good is to be found in pleasure. Pleasure is an unimpeded activity of our natural state (1153a13). If pain is evil, pleasure must be good. Though it is true that many pleasures are relatively rather than absolutely good, and that many become bad if carried to excess (cp. 1148a22 ff), this still does not prevent pleasure in some sense from being the supreme good. This is a surprising statement, and in the tenth book while repeating his refutation of Speusippus he also examines and rejects the view of Eudoxus that pleasure is the supreme good. Eudoxus had argued that all creatures seek pleasure, and seek it as an end in itself; further that pleasure enhances other goods. Aristotle, following Plato, takes this last point to prove that pleasure is *a* good, but not *the* Good. He proceeds to expound his own view. (a) Pleasure is not a process but is complete. It is not like building a temple or going for a walk, but like an act of perception. (b) It arises from any faculty attaining its proper object; the better the faculty the greater the pleasure. (c) It perfects an activity, though distinct from it, as a supervening completion, like the bloom on a ripe peach (1174b32). (d) It cannot be continuously maintained. (e) It is inseparably connected with life. Life is a form of activity, and the pleasure of those activities perfects life. Aristotle rounds off his discussion with a series of carefully drawn distinctions. Pleasures differ in kind, because our activities differ in kind, and each is completed by its peculiar pleasure. Further, particular pleasures may conflict: pleasure in philosophical discussion may conflict with pleasure in overhearing a musician practising (this is one of those moments when we suddenly become aware of Aristotle's class as alive and actual). Pleasures differ according to the moral worth of the activity concerned, according to the animal feeling the pleasure (John Stuart Mill said, "It is better to be Socrates dissatisfied than a pig satisfied"), according to individual taste, and according to the individual's own physical condition.

VIII *Friendship and Happiness*

Aristotle now proceeds to his final examination of happiness. But before we follow him there we must turn back to the two books of apparent digression which deal with friendship. They give us the fullest and most useful extant contemporary treatment of the subject, though Aristotle's successor Theophrastus wrote an important monograph that is reflected in the works of later writers, and though the Epicurean attitude to friendship is notably warm and attractive. Friendship is important to Aristotle because friendliness (the Greek word is the same) is a virtue or involves virtue, and because friendship is an indispensable requisite of life (1155a3). Again we are conscious that to Aristotle, rightly, man is always man in society; we are not isolated atoms. John Burnet has usefully suggested that the logic of Aristotle's arrangement of topics is that friendship represents the altruistic use of practical good sense, paving the way toward the ultimate "intellectual love of God" and bridging the gap between practical and theoretical wisdom.[16] Aristotle sees friendship as profoundly natural; not for him is Thomas Hobbes with his *homo homini lupus* and the essentially predatory character of human relationships. Friendship has its root in the family; it is the cement of society and extends throughout the human race. Friendship is the recognition of mutual goodwill, based on utility, pleasure, or virtue, or a combination of these qualities (1156a3). It will be noticed that friendship for Aristotle embraces business association, political alliance, membership of the same team, as well as a more personal relationship. Friendship based on virtue is the highest and rarest; it alone has permanence; and it cannot be hurried. Friendship based on utility fades when the profit fades, but friendship based on pleasure can be durable. This last includes love-affairs, and Aristotle points out that if they are to last, enjoyment of physical beauty must be transmuted into enjoyment of total personality. Friendship, like the other virtues, is a disposition which needs to be maintained by exercise. Aristotle, though insisting that reciprocity distinguishes friendship from goodwill, says explicitly that friendship seems to consist more in giving than in receiving affection. This is remarkable: Greek ethics, and Aristotle's own thought, tend to be egocentric.

All friendship involves community, and Aristotle explores the social and political aspects of friendship. He anticipates his political classification of constitutions into monarchy, aristocracy, timocracy (or constitutional government), and their degenerate forms tyranny, or dictatorship, oligarchy (the wealthy replace the "best"), and democracy. There are parallels in the family: the relation of father to children is monarchical, of husband and wife aristocratic, i.e., based on merit in appropriate fields ("A wife who is an heiress may exercise the authority" 1161a1), of brothers timocratic. Democracy appears in households where there is no master, or where the master is weak. There is an appropriate form of friendship for each relationship, but in the degenerate forms, except democracy, friendship has no role. Of the constitutions monarchy is the best, timocracy the worst; but of the degenerate forms democracy is the best, tyranny the worst; *corruptio optimi pessima* (cf *Pol.* 1289a40).

The most interesting part of the remaining discussion is the proposition that friendship is based on self-love (1166a1). There are four characteristic marks of friendship: (a) the promotion of another's good for his sake, (b) desire for another's safety for his sake, (c) pleasure in another's society, and (d) sympathy in joy and sorrow. The good man desires his own good and security, likes his own company, and is keenly aware of his own joys and sorrows. Friendship is an extension of this; the friend is proverbially "a second self," and selfhood can be extended to include another. This is a remarkable attempt to expound altruism in terms of an egocentric psychology. But, after all, even the founder of Christianity said, "Thou shalt love thy neighbour *as thyself.*"

Is friendship then necessary for happiness? Aristotle answers "Yes," but his reasoning is cold. Friends are the greatest of external goods. The good man needs friends on whom to practise his beneficence (rather as the believer in Islam needs beggars on whom to practise the virtue of almsgiving). Man needs society; for happiness a man needs to share in the good activities of others, and this helps our own discipline in right action. Sympathy enlarges our consciousness and therefore our happiness. This last is an interesting point. Shelley defended poetry because the great secret of morals is love, the capacity to identify ourselves with others; this requires imagination, and poetry "strengthens the faculty which is the organ of the moral nature of man in the same manner as exercise strengthens a limb." [17] This may be true, but Aristotle does not say this; he says that to enter into the experience of others increases our happiness. In the immediate sense this is not true; it is equally likely to increase our anguish. Either the world-view is overoptimistic, or the choice of friends confined to the prosperous, or the argument needs to be taken to a deeper level. But at the last (1171b29) Aristotle drops his rationalizations and expresses in a tumbling congeries of verbs compounding with *syn* ("together") his sheer joy in togetherness with others.

After the second part of his discussion of pleasure Aristotle finally turns to the consummation of his thinking about the end of man (1176a30). Happiness is not a state or disposition but a self-contained activity. It is not recreational activity, but activity exercising the highest part of our being, the intellect, in accordance with the highest virtue, theoretical wisdom: it is in fact contemplation. Contemplation can be practised continuously; it brings with it remarkable pleasures; it is self-contained; it is an end in itself; and it is possible only by virtue of the divine element in man. We ought then not confine our thoughts to the ephemeral, but so far as possible we ought to seek immortality. The life of moral virtue offers happiness but only in a secondary degree, as it is more dependent on externals. But Aristotle cannot completely immunize the philosopher from the need for external well-being; he hedges by suggesting that his needs are less than those of others.

Aristotle is in continual tension between his doctrine of self-sufficiency and his social ethic. One scholar has suggested that in speaking of self-sufficiency he fluctuates between the meanings of "sufficient" and "sufficient and independent." [18] Of course we are not self-sufficient; we cannot walk a few yards without using that very expensive manufactured article, a street; our food is grown by one group, processed by others, transported by others, sold by others, and they in turn are dependent on yet others for the equipment they use. Even in the far simpler conditions of life in Greece this was true; the approach to independence could never be more than asymptotic. So Aristotle returns at the last to the social environment of ethics. Men attain to virtuous behavior by natural endowment, habituation, training. Training is environmental. The home is important, but it is the state and its laws which are of supreme importance. This leads us straight to politics.

IX *Politics and the Ideal State*

Aristotle's *Politics* as we have it is a compote of three series of lectures, unfinished, disorganized, and clumsily dovetailed. The first three books form an introduction to Political Science. The next three are concerned with Practical Politics. The last two deal with the Ideal State. But there is evidence of continuity between the first and last series. Furthermore, the first three books, although they cohere, are really detached monographs, and there is some evidence that the third book is the oldest of all. Some scholars think that the sixth book should be read before the fifth. The whole matter has been debated at great length.[19] We do well to remember that Aristotle was a teacher, and good teachers do continually revise, expand, and reorganize their courses; they will keep material by them which they know needs rewriting, and may even continue to use it with off-the-cuff modifications; they may use the same material in different combinations and at different lengths for different purposes. Perhaps Aristotle began with a course on the nature of the state (III), and added a course on the history of the search for the ideal state (II). He then may have decided to give the whole subject of political science a more elaborate treatment, and that he needed to preface these courses with a set of lectures on the family unit as the foundation of the state (I) and to complete the historical account of ideal constitutions with his own formula (VII–VIII). But before completing this he decided that he had to expose his students to a more solid grounding in fact, and this led him to incorporate the new set of lectures on Practical Politics (IV–VI). But he was still using the old lectures and never got around to revising and completing them. Some editors rearrange the order of the books; but it is perhaps as well to accept that there is no "right" order, and to treat the work as a series of monographs.

Aristotle begins from the proposition that every city-state is a kind of association (1252a1). It is important to realize from the first his terms of reference. When Aristotle talks of politics, he is thinking of the city-state (*polis*), a unit of strictly limited size formed by the synoecism of a number of villages; later, he says that a nation is too large for a state, and he envisages a unit in which all the citizens can meet in a single assembly. He began his *Ethics*, to which *Politics* is the sequel, with the proposition that all things aim at some good. He now repeats this, and asserts that the city-state is the supreme form of association, and must aim at the supreme good; he is in fact maintaining the teleological approach which he has already laid down. The primary natural partnership is the family, consisting of the head of the house, his wife and servant (slave); so does Aristotle from the outset show the extraordinary mixture of sound scientific observation and grotesque class prejudice to which he was prone. Related households join together to form a village in order to meet their physical needs; villages join in a city-state, the ultimate form of association, because it reaches the goal of self-sufficiency. It comes into being for the sake of life; its real being is for the sake of the good life (1252b30). This is almost to say that its existence precedes its essence. It is a natural growth, and Aristotle proceeds to his celebrated and much mistranslated affirmation, that man is a living creature who naturally lives in city-states; he does not say, at least not without careful definition and qualification, that man is a "political animal" (1253a3). It follows that the city-state is naturally, or, as we might say, logically, prior to the family and to the individual, standing as whole to part. An individual who did not need community would be either a wild animal or a god (1253a29). "He that delighteth in solitude is either a wild beast or a god," said Bacon. It will be noticed that if Aristotle's analysis has any validity, a world in which the state has become bloated and swollen beyond any recognition as a city-state needs units of community in which the individual can genuinely participate and find a fulfilment not provided by our elective aristocracies; further that those who reject Aristotle's view of the political inferiority of "servants" and women must be sure they do not suffer from residual prejudices and are offering an equality that is practical as well as theoretical.

X *Slavery and Economics*

The remainder of the first book is mainly concerned with two topics: slavery and economics. The discussion of slavery is of considerable historical interest; but it is deplorable. It can be said in extenuation that slavery was virtually universal in the ancient world, and Aristotle as a scientist observes and interprets what he sees. Even so, advanced thinkers like Euripides and Alcidamas were already challenging the institution. Aristotle treats the slave as subhuman, a tool, a piece of property, endowed with life; he sees the distinction between ruler and ruled as inherent in nature. Yet he is uneasy; he grants the slave a faculty of reason (1255b21) and elsewhere a capacity for friendship (*Eth.* 1161b5) and the right to look forward to freedom (1330a32). This really makes nonsense of his theory. In practice he sees that by his own standards it is difficult to tell who is the natural slave, and that war and other circumstances (as the Athenian Lycurgus had established in a piece of enlightened legislation) [20] often enslave "the wrong man." One might wish in the computer age to invert his thinking and make real the fullness of participation in community life which release from mechanical drudgery has made possible.

His discussion of economics is to our thinking more advanced. He distinguishes between the direct acquisition of natural products in order to meet basic needs, which is natural, and the pursuit of monetary wealth for its own sake, which is unnatural. The first includes nomadic pasturage and agriculture (the addition of piracy need be no more than a lecturer's joke, though it may be a serious sociological comment); it belongs to the basic structure of family life. To this he is prepared to add the barter of necessary supplies and makes an important distinction between two ways of using an article, say a shoe, one directly by wearing it, and one indirectly as an instrument of exchange (1257a6). Natural economics are limited by our needs. Then money was invented, being (literally) handy for exchange, and created commerce, and from this came the love of money which Paul declared to be the root of all evil, and whose maw is unlimited. Aristotle reserves his severest condemnation for usury; it passed from him to the medieval church, and it required the Protestant revolution to divert Christian-Aristotelian principle in the interests of the emergent business class. Of course Aristotle's analysis is oversimplified, but it is good at times to be recalled to first principles.

At the end of the book he returns to family life. The head of the house rules his slave despotically, his wife constitutionally, his children monarchically; so there is a correlation between family and state, part and whole.

Particular interest in the second book attaches to Aristotle's treatment of Plato. Plato in *The Republic* propounded an ideal state depending on the efficiency of a specialized ruling class. He saw the two disruptive elements as financial corruption and nepotism (the very factors which in the twentieth century disrupted the first Republic of Nigeria), and proposed to eliminate them by communism of property and of family among the ruling class. Aristotle begins by asserting sensibly, but without direct relevance, that unity is not uniformity. His rejection of family communism seems more emotional than rational, but he points out that family affection would be watered down (1262b15). His objection to economic communism is based on *mine* and *yours:* common property is no one's property. Plato, he suggests, fails to see that the problem lies not in institutions but in human wickedness (1263b23). Plato deprives his ruling class of natural happiness, and if they are not happy, who will be? It all sounds rather like a defense of the American way of life! Aristotle voices the stock objections; he may have seen idealistic experiments break up on these practical points. Yet institutions do matter; at the least, a competitive society encourages competition and a cooperative society cooperation. Plato in fact demands less of his rulers than the Catholic church has demanded of its monks, whom they in many ways resemble. And Aristotle does not really provide an alternative answer to the abuses Plato is seeking to eliminate.

He passes to Plato's later work *The Laws* and takes his hearers along a fascinating byway of history into the Utopias of the otherwise unknown Phaleas and the famous architect and town-planner Hippodamus. He ruefully points to a rock which has wrecked many economies since: the moment the underprivileged achieves a measure of "levelling up," the group above them demands differential rewards for skill or responsibility (1266b40). From these theoretical constructions he passes to actual constitutions which have been admired; Sparta, where he criticizes the oppressive serfdom, the freedom of women, the concentration of property into too few hands, the dictatorial power of the five ephors, the exclusive direction of the state to war, and the inefficient taxation; Crete; Carthage; and Solon's constitution at Athens which he rightly sees as reformist rather than revolutionary.

XI *Citizenship and Constitutions*

I have suggested that the third book comprises Aristotle's original course of lectures on political science, and for that reason it is perhaps the best introduction to this thought. The primary element in the city-state is citizens: the truism is only apparent. Citizenship consists not in common residence or blood-relationship, but in direct participation in the deliberative and judicial functions of the community. This excludes resident aliens (there is some circular thinking here; but Aristotle is reporting facts, not defining; it should be remembered that he lived in Athens himself as a disfranchised alien); children (who are citizens in embryo); women (whose personal qualities Aristotle regards as different); slaves (who, apart altogether from Aristotle's prejudices, would be aliens); and members of the working-class. These last were, as he points out, sometimes included. But they have not the leisure for continuous participation in politics, and it is to be feared that he regards them as intellectually unfit for it. Aristotle has all the white-collar prejudices against manual labor. But there is more to it than that. He would not think that a citizen was exercising his citizenship by casting a vote once every four years; he believes firmly in direct government rather than representative government, and that demands time, which everyone (for economic reasons) has not been able to give; his concept of citizenship is thus less extensive but far, far more intensive than modern concepts. It is ironical that the development of the machine has made the Aristotelian ideal possible for all in an age when we care so little about it that we speak of "the problem of leisure."

The rest of the book deals with the classification and analysis of different constitutions. The classification is that which we have met in *Ethics* (1160a31): monarchy, aristocracy, constitutional government with their degenerate forms, tyranny (the dictatorship of the 1930s) oligarchy, democracy. These are obviously distinguished by whether the ruling power is in the hands of one person, a few, or many, but in an aside which illuminates contemporary Greek history Aristotle suggests that in practice oligarchy is government by the rich, democracy government by the poor, and government by a rich majority would still be oligarchy (1279b20; 1290a30 ff; 1317b38). A perceptive section shows that all agree that justice means equality for equals and inequality for unequals. But what is the criterion? Wealth, shout the oligarchs. Freedom, cry the democrats. This sweeps Aristotle into an eloquent affirmation that the state does not exist for trade or military defense but to promote the good life in community, and this capacity, not wealth, birth, or freedom gives the right to political power (1281a4). A certain mood of paternalism will be noted. He returns from ideal to practice, and offers cautious reasons in defense of some democracy: many heads are better than one; exclusion of the masses from government leads to revolutionary discontent; the people can judge the work of the executive, as an occupant can evaluate a house, or a diner a chef, and should have the right of election.

But democracy must be practised within the rule of law; Aristotle is guarding against the inconsistencies of the Athenian assembly. And other merits, especially political excellence (but he adds property, wealth, and birth), have their claims. Aristotle concludes with a long discussion of monarchy, in which there is no direct mention of Macedon, a dangerous topic at Athens. He isolates five types of monarchy: the Spartan (the office of permanent commander in chief); the Oriental; the constitutional dictatorship; the legendary heroic monarchy; absolute sovereignty. The list can be reduced to the first and last. Absolute sovereignty is dangerous, and there is much to be said for the rule of law; but there is nothing unnatural about monarchy as an institution, and where a really exceptional individual is found—and here Aristotle may have had Alexander in mind—it is natural for the community freely to accept him as their sovereign (1288a28).

Books IV–VI, as we have said, deal with practical politics. Aristotle starts from his theoretical classification of constitutions, and it is clear that his notes on aristocracy have been lost (1289a31). But for practical purposes we can concentrate on democracy and oligarchy, the power of the poor and the power of the rich, though this is rather like dividing all the winds into north and south (1290a14). In fact the situation is more complex: Aristotle recognizes eight classes—farmers, industrial workers, businessmen, laborers, military, judiciary, property-owners, civil servants—but these classes may overlap, and the basic intransigent division is between rich and poor. But democracies are of various kinds: there may be genuine political equality between a rich man and a poor man; there may be a low property qualification; there may be equality in office but not under the law; or there may be demagogy, disrespect for law and government by perpetual plebiscite. So too there are varieties of oligarchy from what is almost a limited democracy with a high property assessment to dynastic government by a few powerful families. Aristotle's main object in this book is to set alongside these what he regards as the best form of government in practice, constitutional government (*politeia*). It is a blend of the best aspects of oligarchy and democracy, with a leaning toward democracy (1293b31 ff). It is characterized by the rule of law, and institutions which compromise between democratic and oligarchic practice; thus office might be elective but the basis should not be wealth. It is interesting to recall that Montesquieu also fostered a mixed constitution, but in a very different spirit; his aim was a division of powers, Aristotle's was a union of classes.[21]

After a curiously brief digression on tyranny or dictatorship (1295a1), Aristotle reveals that his real formula for political happiness is a strong middle class, the group which, as Aristotle put it, treats political office as a responsibility rather than as a burden or a means to power, and which tended to be squeezed out by the extreme factions in Greek politics. The view may be dismissed as class prejudice, but Aristotle's ear was close to the ground, and Greece had seen too much of the instability caused by the rival factions of extreme left and extreme right. Aristotle finally examines the typical arrangements made by democracy, oligarchy, aristocracy, and constitutional government over the three main functions of state, deliberative, executive, and judicial.

XII *Revolutions*

The next book has been variously entitled "The Pathology of the State" or "Revolutions—their Cause and Cure." It is a fascinating book for the spotlight it throws on some of the darker corners of Greek political history: we learn of revolutions caused by ethnic troubles, of the difference of political mood between Athens and her port Piraeus, of a revolution arising out of the marriage of two heiresses, of another when a magistrate fined his prospective son-in-law. The theory illustrated by this wealth of historical illustration can be swiftly stated. The material cause of revolution is the distribution of wealth and power; oligarchs think it should be distributed unequally, democrats equally. The final cause of revolution is material profit or prestige, or its negative, rebellion against penury or degradation. The efficient causes of revolution are various, but indignation against some form of inequitable treatment covers most of them (1302a16 ff). Much of the book analyzes these in greater detail in relation to the different types of constitution. A shrewd passage shows how dictators defend their power in two diametrically opposed ways, by repressive measures and by demonstrative beneficence (1313a34 ff). In general the cure for revolution (1307b26 ff) consists in: maintaining the sovereignty of and respect for the law; a genuine concern for the well-being of people (far better than any political gimmickry); unity against an outside enemy (such as America and Russia had against Nazi Germany, or Ibos and Hausas against the British colonial regime in Nigeria); the avoidance of extremes of wealth, power, and privilege; people of loyalty, ability, and integrity to hold office; and a system of education directed toward constructive participation in the life of the community. This sort of practical idealism shows Aristotle at his best; it is still relevant.

XIII *Democracy, Oligarchy, Government Offices, and Education*

Book VI is altogether slighter, though again of historical interest. It falls into two parts. The first examines democracy and oligarchy. The catchwords of democracy are shrewdly presented: liberty; the right to government and be governed in turn; political equality without respect to merit (or as we would say "One man one vote," a major issue in twentieth century Rhodesia or South Africa); "Live as *you* like." So to their political corollaries; election of officials by all from all; government of each by all and of all by each in turn; election by lot; no property qualifications; no office normally to be held twice by the same person; short tenure of office; judicial functions exercised by the whole people; the sovereignty of the assembly; remuneration for public duties (1317a40). It is a brilliantly succinct picture of direct democracy. In his extended analysis Aristotle shows his usual revulsion from extremes. The analysis of oligarchy (1320b18) is slighter, but the observation that oligarchy is maintained by military power and will be more durable if office is seen to be expensive rather than lucrative and if the commons share in communal prosperity, is shrewd enough.

The second part (1321b4) is little more than an enumeration of the offices of government. They fall into three groups. The essential offices are: superintendent of markets; superintendent of highways and buildings; superintendent of land and forests; revenue officers; recorders; superintendent of prisons. The prestigious offices are: military boards; auditors; executive council; religious officials. The third group is optional and found in prosperous states, e.g., minister for women; guardian of the laws; minister for children; minister for sport; and the like. These pages bring home to us the actualities of the Greek city-state, and remind us how deeply Aristotle's thought was rooted in those actualities.

The last two books are a general treatise on the ideal state. Aristotle goes back to the point he has established in *Ethics;* happiness is found in the life of virtue. If this is true in private life it must be true politically; even the mastery of the world would be unenviable without virtue; what profit to gain the whole world and lose your own soul? And as the highest virtue for the individual lies in the contemplative life, so in the state it may lie in the internal life of the community rather than in a busy interventionism. This established, Aristotle passes to external conditions and makes it again clear that he is still thinking of the limited city-state, in the days when Alexander was sweeping across half the world. First, population. A state is to be judged by efficiency, not size; it must have enough for well-being, but not so many that they cannot meet in a single assembly. Second, territory. This should give economic self-sufficiency without luxury. Aristotle is acutely aware of the advantages and disadvantages of access to the sea, both clearly revealed in the history of Athens, where a strong navy had, for good or ill, fostered alien immigration, economic and political imperialism, and radical democracy. Third, race. Aristotle suggests that the Europeans have drive without intelligence, the Asiatics intelligence without drive, and the Greeks the best of both worlds. The Hippocratic doctors made some study of the influence of climate on character, and no doubt it was from them that Aristotle derived the thought; it is again reminiscent of Montesquieu.

Aristotle now moves to organization. There are six essential activities in a community: food-supply; industry; arms; finance; religion; justice. This is the basis of class division, but it can be simplified. Aristotle is not a democrat, except cautiously and pragmatically. He is a snob, but also a political realist; he sees that political, economic, and military power cannot be divorced, and suggests that the same group should form the army in their youth, the administration in their prime, and the priesthood in their old age, and that they should be the propertied class. This view takes off from Plato, who started with a class of soldier-rulers who are the repository of wisdom, but Aristotle does not require of his rulers economic and sexual self-abnegation. He allows for a private and public sector in land ownership. There are some interesting details of town-planning, which should be designed with an eye to fresh air, water supply, administration, and war. Aristotle comes to terms with the grid plan, but something more complex is militarily better, as the curving streets of Boston were said to allow the settlers to cope with the Indians. Some of his provisions again reflect his medical interests, and Hippocratic research.

The remainder of *Politics* deals with education. Virtue is the product of nature, habit, and reason (1332a40), and habit and reason require education. Education is ultimately training for leisure (a lesson we have not wholly learned). It is training of the whole man, and the disciplines of the body and of the emotions and will lead to the training of the mind and the *psyche*. Aristotle starts from eugenic provisions (he favors marriage at thirty-seven for the male, eighteen for the female). There are three stages in education, roughly the ages 0–7, 8–14, 15–21. In the first there should be a milk diet without much wine, a gradual inuring to toughness, games which pave the way to serious pursuits, and great care about the child's environment. Aristotle is not against a few tears; they are good exercise. So far education has been in the home. In the second period formal schooling starts, and Aristotle holds very strongly that it should be state-controlled; it is too important to be left to private enterprise. The traditional curriculum embraced reading and writing; physical training; and music and literature; with drawing sometimes added. Unfortunately, Aristotle's discussion is incomplete and somewhat unsystematic. But he makes one very important point. If leisure is the end or aim, then it cannot be merely recreational; we should train for its constructive use, and this is the real place of music and literature (1338b22). So after briefly discussing the object of physical training, which should be directed to physical fitness not to the cult of athletic sports, he turns at some length to the place of music in education. It has its place as relaxation, as an instrument of moral education (the Greeks were interested in the capacity of music to draw out an emotional response. Some music made Boswell feel like plunging into the thick of battle. "Sir," said Dr. Johnson, "if it made me feel such a fool I should not hear it"), and as intellectual pastime. That a treatise on man in society should tail away in the middle of a discussion of music might seem at first odd, but it is typical of Aristotle's comprehensive outlook and his attention to detail.

XIII *Summary*

Three things cannot fail to strike us upon this part of Aristotle's work. The first is that to him man means man in society. *Politics* restores the balance which was lost at the end of *Ethics* in which we were confronted with the figure of the solitary thinker. A man finds his fulfillment only in community, a community of living together. His well-being alike contributes to and depends upon the well-being of that community. "No man is an *Iland,* intire of it selfe; every man is a peece of the *Continent,* a part of the *maine,*" wrote John Donne in another context, and though Donne's vision was more widely embracing, the truth it enshrines is the same.[22]

Secondly, Aristotle's political vision seems to us at first blow incredibly parochial, limited as it is to the Greek city-state at the very threshold of the imperial age. He has, it seems, no vision of the nation-state, still less of a great federation like the United States. But is he so parochial? We have come to appreciate the concept of optimal size in industry, in schools and colleges, in airports (O'Hare and Kennedy have long passed it). We have scarcely begun to apply it to politics. The Greek world may have been broken by war, but European nationalism can claim no better record. It is not unimportant that the one really successful experiment in centralized government of a wide area in the western world, the Roman Empire, which gave to a larger area of the globe a longer period of untroubled peace than at any time before or since, depended for its success upon the self-governing municipality, which was virtually the Greek city-state. Perhaps we have something to learn from Aristotle after all.

Finally, as Renford Bambrough puts it: "Once again we notice the importance to Aristotle of the description of *how things are* as an essential element in any reflection on *how things ought to be.* In the later books, when he makes his own proposals for an ideal community, he is as down-to-earth, as directly concerned with the light that the actual concrete specimens can throw on the abstract consideration of the formal and the ideal, as in his works on biology, ethics, and literature."[23]

CHAPTER 9

Rhetoric and Poetics

"THE *Rhetoric* of Aristotle is a practical psychology, and the most helpful book extant for writers of prose and for speakers of every sort." So Lane Cooper, startlingly, in 1932, and others have been found to echo the judgment.[1] For human nature changes depressingly little, and the principles of persuasion remain unaltered. Ross was less favorable, characterizing the work as "a curious jumble of literary criticism with second-rate logic, ethics, politics, and jurisprudence, mixed by the cunning of one who knows well how the weaknesses of the human heart are to be played upon."[2] In fact, Aristotle with his far-ranging mind, and rare combination of analysis and synthesis, treats his theme with perspicacity. In 1810 Edward Copleston in defending the University of Oxford against its critics found himself writing in defense of Aristotle, and included a judicious evaluation of his *Rhetoric.*[3] He calls it "a magazine of intellectual riches," points to its accurate and luminous arrangement, notes that it is founded on a close knowledge of human nature, political history past and contemporary, and the writing of poets and orators, and includes, "The whole is a textbook of human feeling; a storehouse of taste; an exemplar of condensed and accurate, but uniformly clear and candid, reasoning."

I *Kinds of Oratory*

"Rhetoric is the counterpart of dialectic" (1354a1). Aristotle does not begin with a definition, but with a general statement on the nature of rhetoric; public speaking and logical discussion are different but related disciplines. Rhetoric is a discipline, a science, though one might not think so, says Aristotle, from the current textbooks which concentrate on inessentials and tend to deal with forensic rather than political oratory. Rhetoric is important because (a) it can prevent the natural triumph of truth and justice from being obstructed, (b) it can persuade a non-intellectual audience where intellectual demonstration fails, (c) it ensures that we look at both sides of a question, (d) it is an essential weapon of self-defense. (This last throws a shaft of light on Greek public life.) Rhetoric then is the capacity for discovering the practicable methods of persuasion in a given case (1355b26). Methods of persuasion may be rhetorical or non-rhetorical. Rhetorical factors are three: the personal character of the speaker, the mood induced in the audience, and the arguments. A public speaker must thus be a sound logician, familiar with characteristic attitudes of mind, and sensitive to emotional response. In dialectic, induction and the syllogism are the two tools of the logician; corresponding to these the public speaker has the example and the enthymeme. Aristotle discusses the enthymeme in the second book (1393a21 ff). Here we may note that it is a persuasive argument which, if reduced to strict logical form, would become a syllogism. When Dick Dudgeon in Shaw's *The Devil's Disciple,* facing execution, says to the chaplain "Thou shalt not kill," it is a form of enthymeme. Aristotle says, a trifle naïvely, "Speeches which rely on examples are just as persuasive, but those which rely on enthymemes are more warmly applauded." (1356b22). The orator deals in generalizations and probabilities, and because his audience consists of men-in-the-street (the jury in the law-courts and the voters in the political assembly) he will abbreviate his argument. Alongside probabilities are "signs": heavy breathing is a sign of fever.

There are three branches of rhetoric, that of the political assembly, that of the law courts, and that of the ceremonial occasion. In each the speaker is concerned with pros and cons, relating respectively to expediency, justice, and honor, and he needs a stock of propositions on these three topics. The political orator is concerned mainly with five topics: (a) income and expenditure, (b) war and peace, (c) national defense, (d) imports and exports, and (e) legislation. The goal he holds before his audience is happiness, a combination of prosperity and virtue, which Aristotle analyzes into a noble heritage from the past, children, wealth, fame, honor, bodily vigor, a good old age, friends, good luck, and virtue. Next comes an analysis of things called good: happiness, the virtues, physical qualities, wealth, friends, honor, the capacity to speak and to act, intellectual gifts, life, justice. (These, it is to be feared, are the things to which politicians pay lip service.) Of course there are problems. Good rules are: good is the opposite of evil; excess is likely to be evil; the object of general competition is likely to be good; the object pursued by a man who has won our respect is likely to be good. This leads to a prolix comparison of good objects with one another. Much of the discussion is inconclusive: in one sense a rare object is better, as gold is more precious than iron, in another a common object, as iron, is more useful than gold (1364a23). Finally, the political orator must be familiar with the several types of constitution: democracy, which promotes freedom; oligarchy, which promotes wealth; aristocracy, which promotes rational traditions; constitutional monarchy; and dictatorship, which promotes the interests of the dictator.

Aristotle then briefly discusses the scope of epideictic oratory, the oratory of the formal occasion. This is concerned with the praiseworthy, and particularly with moral excellence, which he analyzes into nine components: justice, courage, self-discipline, magnificence, nobility, liberality, good temper, practical good sense, theoretical wisdom; the list includes the four "cardinal" virtues, but is not as full as the list in *Ethics;* Aristotle does not profess to be offering a full discussion. With strong practicality he points out that a panegyrist or a critic may exaggerate his subject's virtues or vices, and identify his qualities with those a little up or down the scale: cautious=calculating; thick-skinned=good humored: quick-tempered=frank; arrogant=dignified; rash=brave; extravagant=open-handed; Aristotle was not without a sense of humor.

So to forensic oratory: prosecution and defense. Wrongdoing is voluntary action, contrary to law (written or unwritten), causing harm; it arises from vice or from weakness of will. All human action springs from one of seven causes: chance, nature, compulsion, habit, reason, anger, or desire. Further, all voluntary actions are directed to expediency or pleasure. Pleasure is movement by which the *psyche* is brought into its natural state; pleasures may consist in memory of the past, enjoyment of the present, or anticipation of the future. Aristotle lists pleasures, starting, oddly, with revenge, and proceeds to victory and hence to competition, fame, friendship, admiration, familiarity, variety, learning and intellectual curiosity, giving and receiving favors, fine art, birds of one's own feather, wisdom, criticizing one's neighbors, doing our own thing, enjoyment of the ridiculous. It is a gloriously miscellaneous catalog. He returns more closely to the problems of the law courts. A criminal will not act unless he believes that the crime can be successfully committed, that he can commit it successfully, that he will not be found out, or, if found out, will escape punishment, or, if punished, will gain more than he loses. Typical criminals are those who trust in their own eloquence or riches to get them off, those who are unlikely to be suspected (a weakling of assault and battery, an ugly pauper of adultery), those who have the cheek to commit their crimes openly or on a large enough scale, those who have got away with it in their past, those with a good enough reputation to escape suspicion, or a bad enough one not to mind it. They may offend against written or unwritten law, that is local or universal law, legality or equity.

In the last chapter of the first book Aristotle reverts to non-rhetorical factors in persuasion. These are five: laws (the orator may appeal from legality to equity, or insist on legality, as suits his case); witnesses alike to the facts, the character of the defendant, and the nature of the case (if you have no witnesses, argue from probabilities, which cannot be bribed; if your case is implausible, rely on witnesses); contracts (insist on them, if they favor you; discredit them if they do not); torture, the normal method of extracting evidence from a slave (if it favors you, it is reliable; if not, people will say anything to escape pain); oaths (you must decide (a) whether to exact an oath from your opponent, or (b) whether to take one yourself). It is altogether an amusing backstage glimpse at Athenian legal methods.

Aristotle has broken off his treatment of the rhetorical factors for this appendix. He now returns to the rhetorical factors, but for the moment abandons the logical arguments, and after a brief recapitulation begins the second book with his other factors of character and emotional mood. In a swift summary he deals with both. The persuasiveness of a speaker will depend (a) upon his establishing an impression of good sense, good moral character, and good will, and (b) upon his evoking appropriately from his hearers the emotions of anger, pity, fear, and the like. Aristotle now embarks on an elaborate analysis of emotional moods: anger, the desire to avenge a slight (contempt, spite, or gross insult), to be evoked on the jury against one's opponent; mildness; friendship; hostility; fear (a pain or disturbance due to a mental picture of prospective evil); confidence; shame (a pain or disturbance relating to evils, past, present, or future, which may be discreditable to us); shamelessness; benevolence (an attitude of helpfulness towards someone in need); indifference; pity (pain at the sight of unmerited ill fortune, which is not felt by those in extreme prosperity or adversity, nor towards those very close to us or very far from us); indignation (pain at the sight of unmerited good fortune, which may be used as a counter to pity); envy; emulation; contempt.

This completes the discussion of emotional mood. Aristotle then turns to the factor of character, though not as we expect the character of the speaker but the character of the audience in whom he is to induce an emotional response. He analyzes character first in relation to age, and begins with a brilliant account of what we should today call the character of the college student (1389a2); dominated by sex, impulsive, combative, more interested in glory than in money, ready to believe in human nature, optimistic, gullible, idealistic, delighting in fellowship, having all the answers, tending to absolute positions, warm and free from malice. By contrast, the elderly are cautious, conservative, cynical, small-minded, acquisitive, self-centered, living in the past, calculating, ready to pity not out of warmth but out of their own weakness, and querulous. It is only in the prime of life that men show a proper balance of positive qualities. Aristotle also discusses the effect on character of birth, wealth, power, and fortune, all tending to produce an attitude of superiority, though the last is sometimes accompanied by piety, as men like to attribute their prosperity to divine favor rather than to chance.

Aristotle now turns to list the four basic topics or commonplaces of oratory: (a) the possible and impossible (note, for example, that if one of two contraries is possible, so is the other: if a man can get well he can also fall ill; again if the whole is possible, so is a part of it), (b) the past (the special province of forensic oratory), (c) the future (the special province of political oratory), (d) magnitude, importance, superiority (the special province of epideictic oratory). The treatment seems desultory and summary, and perhaps represents notes for an introductory or elementary short lecture.

Next follows a fuller treatment of example and enthymeme. Examples may be drawn from history or fiction, and the latter may be from traditional lore, like the animal fables of Aesop and Africa, or it may be the speaker's own invention, like Socrates's comparison of the use of lot to choose public officials with the use of lot to choose an athletic team or the captain of a ship. The maxim is a particular kind of enthymeme; it is a generalized statement about practical conduct, implying a particular conclusion; good examples are the familiar "Know yourself" and "Avoid excess." Maxims win approval from popular audiences; they must be answered by appeal to instances to which they patently do not apply ("There can be no excess in abominating crooks"). The enthymeme proper is in Aristotle's view, as we have noted, an abbreviated syllogism. Basically, he makes these three points: (a) there is danger in elaboration, (b) the speaker must himself have the facts at his fingertips, (c) enthymemes may be used for demonstration or for refutation. Considering the weight which Aristotle sets upon the enthymeme his treatment of it seems a little perfunctory; more is to come, but it seems to come incidentally.

The rest of the book reads like a series of miscellaneous notes, which may be what it is. First he returns to "topics" (commonplaces or lines of argument) and now lists twenty-eight: (i) opposites e.g., from war to peace; (ii) inflections e.g., from justly to just; (iii) correlation, e.g., if it is honorable to sell the tax contract it is honorable to buy it; (iv) a fortiori, e.g., if the gods are not omniscient neither are men; (v) time; (vi) hoisting an opponent with his own petard; (vii) definition; (viii) ambiguity; (ix) logical division, e.g., all crime comes from one of three motives and none of them applies to my case; (x) induction; (xi) appeal to precedent; (xii) argument from the parts to the whole; (xiii) argument from consequences; (xiv) argument from consequences of alternative courses of action, e.g., do not be a public speaker—if you speak honestly, men will loathe you, if dishonestly, the gods will loathe you; (xv) the contrast between appearance and reality; (xvi) mathematical parallels; (xvii) argument from identical consequences to identical antecedents; (xviii) circumstances alter cases; (xix) isolating one possible motive as real; (xx) incentives and deterrents; (xxi) incredible occurrences; (xxii) inconsistencies in the opponent's case; (xxiii) meeting slander with fact, e.g., the woman kissing a lad was not his mistress but his mother; (xxiv) argument from cause to effect; (xxv) alternative proposal; (xxvi) inconsistency with past commitment; (xxvii) previous mistakes; (xxviii) play on names (Aristotle's first example, from Sophocles, has a modern ring, since Sidero = steely = Stalin).

Next comes a list of nine fallacious lines of argument: (i) diction, whether ambiguity of argument or of single words; (ii) asserting of the whole what is true of the parts and vice versa (The examples do not hang together, but one instance is "Thrasybulus put down thirty dictators"; this sounds like thirty separate achievements); (iii) the use of righteous indignation without argument; (iv) generalization from single instances; (v) treatment of the accidental as essential; (vi) false argument from conclusion to premiss, e.g., all rakes dress smartly—X dresses smartly, therefore he is a rake; (vii) *post hoc* and *propter hoc;* (viii) omission of particular circumstances relevant to the case; (ix) confusion of the universal and the particular.

Finally, apart from a brief appendix, Aristotle asks how to meet enthymemes. There are two methods: (a) one enthymeme may be countered by another, (b) the enthymeme itself may be challenged. This last may be done in four ways: (i) by attacking the premiss, (ii) by adducing a similar premiss with a contrary conclusion, (iii) by adducing a contrary premiss, (iv) by citing precedents to the contrary. We are reminded that enthymemes are drawn from four sources: probabilities, examples, infallible "signs," and ordinary signs.

II *Style and Arrangement in Oratory and Poetry*

This really concludes Aristotle's formal treatment, but he fortunately added a separate treatise of considerable interest, dealing with style and arrangement, and cobbled it on to the other books. Facts, presentation of the facts in words, delivery—these are the three elements of oratory. Aristotle with some historical perspicacity points out that stylistic questions attracted poets before prose writers, and pays a tribute to Gorgias's pioneering work in prose, though finding his style inappropriately poetic. Style should be clear and appropriate. Clarity is achieved by a direct, simple, current vocabulary, but a touch of the exotic is needed to sustain interest: words are like men, and we are interested in foreigners. Appropriateness means something between slangy conversationalism and highflown grandiloquence, both inappropriate. But the speaker with an ear for the occasion lets his style rise and fall imperceptibly on either side of the mean as his theme moves higher or lower.

Aristotle discusses embellishments, metaphor and simile, epithets and diminutives. Such embellishments carry dangers. The main faults of style are four: (a) overelaboration of compound words (commoner in Greek than English, though Shakespeare and Gerald Manley Hopkins offer plenty of examples, appropriate enough, in Aristotle's view, to poetry); (b) the use of archaic or foreign words; (c) overuse of epithets (a thoroughly sound piece of criticism); (d) inappropriate metaphors (Aristotle oddly disapproves of Gorgias's brilliant "In shame you sowed, in misery harvested"; one wonders what he would have to say of Boyle Roche's "I smell a rat; I see him floating in the air, ah! but I shall nip him in the bud"). We return to positive analysis. Good style depends on precise and accurate use of language; on knowing how and when to amplify; on propriety and proportion; on rhythm (a sustained metrical pattern, such as dedecorates pages of *Martin Chuzzlewit,* is to be avoided) especially in the sentence-cadence; on control of the sentence (Aristotle prefers the controlled "periodic" style to the freer style of Herodotus and notes the part played by antithesis, balance, and assonance between phrases in holding the sentence together); on liveliness, contributed by metaphor, especially personification ("Well may Greece cut her hair in mourning at the grave of the fallen"), by visual imagery, by epigram, by the unexpected twist ("Along he minced, wearing on his feet—chilblains"); by puns ("Baring—*Anaschetos* —is past bearing"); by hyperbole (of a man with a black eye: "You would have taken him for a basket of mulberries"). Aristotle concludes the section on style by noting that different styles are appropriate to different circumstances: thus a work available for reading later, like a panegyric, will need to be more polished than an occasional speech; a debating speech will require a strong dramatic element; a plea before a single magistrate will be less rhetorical than one before a large jury.

We now pass to arrangement. Basically, a speech has two parts: you must state your case and you must prove it (1414a13). Aristotle is chary of elaborate analysis, or of generalizing from one kind of speech. All speeches require an introduction. This has two functions: it must grip the attention of the audience and lay the subject before it. An orator may at an early stage have occasion to dispel—or disseminate—prejudice, but this is not a necessary stage. Next will follow the statement. In forensic speeches this consists in a narrative of the facts. Such a narrative, at least in prosecution, will be leisured and extended. It should play on the jury's emotions and lead them imperceptibly to make moral judgments. Third come the arguments, including the refutation of the opponent, and his interrogation where appropriate; Aristotle quotes a good saying of Gorgias, "Meet a serious point with a joke, and joke with a serious point."[4] Finally, the peroration, which has four functions: (a) to win the audience's sympathy, (b) to emphasize your strong points and minimize the weak ones, (c) to work up the audience to an appropriate emotional state, (d) to recapitulate the essential facts. Aristotle favors a direct, straightforward conclusion: "I have done. You have heard. You have the facts. Give your verdict" (1420b4).

III "The Poetics"

The book we know as *The Poetics* — today we would call it perhaps *Creative Writing*—is compact and pithy. It consists of some ten thousand words. In 1570 it took Castelvetro about 384,000 words to expound it; even in the less spacious days of 1957 Gerald Else used nearly the same number. Although Aristotle's theme is creative writing in general, the work as we have it concentrates on tragedy: it is probable that a parallel discussion of comedy has been lost. Aristotle establishes in his introduction that creative writing is concerned with representation (*mimesis*). The word does not mean crude imitation. The Greeks were familiar with such art and told anecdotes of the rivalry of painters in producing *trompe-l'oeil* works, grapes which the birds pecked, a cloth which a rival thought a real cover to the painting. This is not what Aristotle means by *mimesis*. Elsewhere he describes music as a peculiarly mimetic art. He is not thinking of Vaughan Williams's *The Lark Ascending*, Honegger's *CPR*, or the duck in Prokofiev's *Peter and the Wolf;* rather he is thinking of the spirit of the thing. Plato has a long analysis of the relation of mode to mood. Aristotle's representation is this, a Kokoschka portrait not a Madame Tussaud waxwork. The conception is a profound one, profounder when we realize that the object represented is man in action. This established, Aristotle's distinctions seem somewhat formal and mechanical. Tragedy is distinguished from comedy because its characters are noble rather than low; it is distinguished from epic because its presentation is histrionic not narrative, it uses a variety of metres, and it is by its very nature limited in length. (Plays like *Back to Methusaleh* or *The Iceman Cometh* strain the possibilities of the theater to breaking-point.)

It must be remembered that Aristotle is a scientist, and his procedure is scientific. He must have seen hundreds of tragedies; his friend Theodectes produced some fifty plays. His reading probably extended into thousands. Aristotle is first and foremost concerned with what works in the theater; his two favorite plays, *King Oedipus* and *Iphigeneia Among the Taurians* are superbly theatrical. His method is the scientific method of collecting and examining successful plays (not in the crude sense of prize-winning plays, for it was in any case sets of plays which won prizes) and generalizing from them. It is true that he appears to make his generalizations from first principles, but this is common scientific procedure: to start from observations, but to relate the results of observations to more fundamental principle.

Aristotle's definition of tragedy is of great importance. "Tragedy is the representation of an action which is serious, complete in itself, and of a certain limited length; it is expressed in speech beautified in different ways in different parts of the play; it is acted not merely recited; and by exciting pity and fear it produced relief from such emotions" (1449b23). The sturdy practicality of the definition is notable. It is an analysis of the best Greek plays. There have been successful plays which have not conformed to these criteria. Maeterlinck, Shaw, Samuel Beckett, in different ways, have produced plays which did not center on action; Aristotle would have thought them aberrations. *Huis Clos* or *Les Enfants du Paradis* depend upon the fact that the action is incomplete; life goes on in *Huis Clos* to eternity. Still, these are exceptions, protests, experiments. That Aristotle's starting-point is familiarity with his own drama is seen more clearly in the heightening of speech. Probably even the crudest and frankest language must be thus heightened for dramatic purposes; witness LeRoi Jones. But Aristotle has in mind the different rhythms of dialogue and choral lyric; and this is a parochial feature of Greek tragedy. It is really only at the end that a judgment appears which goes beyond the straightforward sifting of data. This is the celebrated theory of *catharsis.*

Fear and pity are related, yet in a sense contradictory. Aristotle defines fear elsewhere as a painful or troubled feeling caused by the impression of an imminent evil (*Rhet.* 1382a20) and pity as a kind of pain excited by the spectacle of evil suffered unmeritedly (1385b12); but those who feel fear should be too preoccupied with themselves to feel pity. Hence, some have understood Aristotle in terms of the contrast between the two, and the subsequent balance. So I. A. Richards: pity is the impulse to advance, fear to retreat; the combination creates an emotional balance. Or James Joyce: pity unites us with the sufferer, fear with the cause; both arrest the mind and raise it in a static state above desire and loathing. Others have seen the one supervening upon the other, so that pain is succeeded by relief. So Freytag: we fear, then our fear turns to pity as we realize we are not involved and cry, "There but for the grace of God go I." Others have interpreted Aristotle's dictum by means of modern psychological theory, whether in terms of root-situations and archetypal images, or the expiation of our unconscious guilt. Browning thought that pity and fear applied to the massive happenings on the stage enabled us to reduce our own petty misfortunes to their proper proportions; Nietzsche, on the contrary, thought we take a malicious satisfaction in the spectacle of cosmic ruin. Others, taking a very different scale, have seen the excitement of the emotions aroused by the play as a kind of inoculation against their occurrence in real life.

These are ingenious and impressive speculations. None is what Aristotle means. This can be discerned by paying attention to the word *catharsis.* The word can bear three meanings: "clarification," "purification," and "purgation." Leon Golden has argued for the meaning "clarification of such pitiable and fearful incidents," but he has had to import a nonexistent previous reference to "pitiable and fearful incidents" to make a plausible rendering. The rendering "purification" was long accepted, and has been defended by reference to a passage in *Ethics* which stresses the importance of feeling pity, fear, and other emotions "at the right time, in the right conditions towards the right people, with the right motive, and in the right way" (1106b21). Nonetheless, there can be little doubt that the real meaning is "purgation"; a passage from *Politics* with direct reference to the purgation of pity and fear through music makes this as clear as may be (1342a7). Pity and fear are undesirable to Aristotle and to all who push their search for self-sufficiency and nonattachment to its logical conclusion. Tragedy acts as an aperient and purges the personality of them.

Two aspects of this highly original view must be noted. First, it is directed against Plato. Plato held that tragedy causes emotional debility, and Aristotle's answer contradicted this view. Further, though the meaning of *catharsis* is "purgation," the overtones of "purification" are there. This is a reassertion of an Apollonian view of creative writing over against Plato's Dionysiac ecstasy. Second, Aristotle is not saying that purgation is the aim of tragedy: as a matter of fact he says that the enjoyment of tragedy lies through pity and fear: the fact that these emotions are purged out of the system is his social defense of tragedy.

Aristotle proceeds to the analysis of tragedy into plot, character, diction, thought, music, and spectacle. Of these he regards plot as by far the most important. He calls it the *psyche* of tragedy; the word is usually rendered "soul" but it clearly means "life" (1450a38). He means that without a plot a play would not move; character alone does not make a play. As far as we can see it was Aristotle who isolated the concept of the plot; the word (*mythos*) meant "myth" or "legend," and Aristotle applied it to the aspect of the legend (for most Greek tragedies dealt in familiar tales) selected by the dramatist and its organization for the stage. Thus when Aristotle says that a play should have a beginning, a middle, and an end, he is not being platitudinous. Legends are not so tidily structured. The word "poet" means literally "maker," and the plot is what he makes by selecting his beginning, middle, and end; the creative writer in this way creates the plot.

The most moving constituents of the plot are *peripeteia* and *anagnorisis*. For the first of these there is no English equivalent. It does not mean, as it is often rendered, merely "reversal of fortune." A *peripeteia* takes place when a course of action designed to produce one result produces its diametrical opposite. The messenger comes to cheer Oedipus and remove his fears, but in revealing who he is has the opposite effect (1452a23). F. L. Lucas has made an eloquent defense of Aristotle's judgment at this point as springing from a full tragic philosophy of life.[5] "For the deepest tragedy is not when men are struck down by the blow of chance or fate like Job or Maurya in *Riders to the Sea* nor yet when they are destroyed by their enemies like Polyxena or Henry VI; but when their destruction is the work of those that wish them well or of their own unwitting hands. For it is the perpetual tragic irony of the Tragedy of Life that again and again men do thus laboriously contrive their own annihilation, or kill the thing they love. When Dejanira, sending her husband the love philtre which was to win him back, poisons him so that he dies cursing her; when Oedipus runs headlong into the jaws of the very destiny from which he is fleeing; when Barabas falls into his own boiling cauldron; when Othello at last sees himself as one who has flung away like an ignorant savage the priceless jewel of his happiness; when Macbeth is lured by the equivocations of the devil to make his own perdition sure; when Lear delivers himself into the hands of the two daughters that despise him and torments the only one that loves—all these are *peripeteias* in the true sense of Aristotle. For the most poignant tragedy of human life is the work of human blindness—the Tragedy of Errors."

Anagnorisis is rightly rendered "recognition," but is not confined to recognition of people, as the recognition of Orestes by Iphigeneia or Oedipus by Jocasta; it is in a wider sense a change from ignorance to knowledge, as with Heracles waking from his madness, Theseus discovering the innocence of Hippolytus, Oedipus's arrival at self-knowledge. To Aristotle the finest plots bring *peripeteia* and *anagnorisis* together; thus this explains his admiration for *King Oedipus* and *Iphigeneia Among the Taurians*, which are in every other way as different as chalk from cheese.

Closely linked with this is the concept of *hamartia*, tragic error. Much, too much, has been made of this by some critics. In Aristotle it is hardly more than an *obiter dictum*, and if it had really been a carefully worked out doctrine central to his tragic philosophy, he would assuredly have elaborated it. The word simply means "missing the target," it does not mean "sinfulness," though the failure may be culpable; indeed Aristotle goes out of his way to distinguish *hamartia* from moral offense (1453a9). Thyestes's error was not his usurpation or his adultery but his ignorance that he was eating his children; Oedipus's error was not the proud imperious temper, but his ignorance of who he was. The error is linked with the climax of the drama; it is this which is revealed at the *anagnorisis*. But Aristotle is offering not a philosophy of life, only a dramatic device.

In a characteristically commonsensical but not quite comprehensive analysis of plots Aristotle accepts two principles of analysis, first, whether the plot moves toward happiness or disaster (a tragedy is a representation of a serious action, and need not have an unhappy ending); second, the character of the protagonist. He finds disaster befalling a saint repellent, success befalling a scoundrel worst of all, disaster befalling a scoundrel deficient in the self-identification of the audience needed to elicit pity and fear. The best plot is when the central character is not morally outstanding and moves to disaster, but not through moral fault. Aristotle has no hesitation in preferring the plot with the unhappy ending, and on these grounds calls Euripides "with all his faults, the most tragic of the creative writers" (1453a29). Aristotle allows, but does not deeply approve, the interweaving of two plots. Plainly all this is based on a solid examination of actual plays.

On character Aristotle makes four points. First, character should be good; it should be remembered that Aristotle's standards are pagan not Christian: the meek do not inherit the world of the theater; further, he has already rejected the perfect hero. Second, they should be true to type; it is to be feared that Aristotle has stereotypes of women, slaves, and other groups in his mind. Rymer condemned Shakespeare's drawing of Iago under a similar head; soldiers are honest. Third, they should be true to tradition; it would not, as Lucas puts it, do to portray Jeremiah as a buoyant optimist, or Herod with a passion for children. Fourth, they should be consistent. Aristotle would not have accepted the sudden conversions of Restoration comedy, and cites Iphigeneia in *Iphigeneia at Aulis* (wrongly, since she is portrayed with tender realism, and her initial nervousness before death is fully understandable) on these grounds.

At this point Aristotle becomes oddly miscellaneous; his usually carefully organized thought falls apart. It is clear that he feels that his original contribution lies in the analysis of plot; he continually reverts to this. There is an extended section on diction, starting from an account of elementary grammar. The best diction is clear without being cheap. On thought, he regards it sufficient to refer back to *Rhetoric*, though he adds that thought should be expressed in action as well as in words. On music and spectacle there is virtually nothing. A comparison of epic with tragedy is of some interest. Aristotle prefers tragedy, as containing all the elements of epic with music and spectacle added, and as being more compact and tautly organized.

It is almost certain, on the basis of a broken manuscript of about 1300, that Aristotle went on to discuss comedy. The discussion was lost in the Dark Ages, but there is a reasonable probability that its outline exists in another fragment called *Tractatus Coislinianus*. The definition there is parallel to that of tragedy: "Comedy is a representation of an action that is ludicrous and defective, of sufficient size; (it is expressed in speech) beautiful in different ways in different parts of the play; it is acted not merely recited; and by exciting pleasure and laughter it produces relief from the comic emotions. Comedy has laughter for its mother." [6] There follows a solidly based analysis of the different devices used to exude laughter. These may be verbal: such as homonyms or puns; synonyms, like Churchill's "terminological inexactitude" for "lie"; garrulity (Dogberry in *Much Ado*); paronyms, or the invention of new words on the basis of existing words; diminutives ("sweet little Socrates" in *The Clouds*); the perversion of words by voice or gesture; the abuse of grammar. Sometimes the humor lies in the theme rather than the words: the assimilation of the worse to the better, or vice versa; deception; the impossible; the possible but inconsequent; the unexpected; debasement of individuals; ludicrous dancing; making a wrong choice; a disjointed story. Comedy requires laughter in proportion, as tragedy requires fear. The constituent parts of comedy are the same as those of tragedy. Typical comic characters are the buffoon, the ironical, the impostor. Thought may be analyzed into opinion and persuasion, persuasion into oaths, agreements, testimonies, ordeals, and laws. Diction for comedy is in the popular idiom, aliens (like the Scythian in *The Thesmophoriazusae*) speaking appropriately. If this analysis is not Aristotle's, it is certainly the work of one who has a sound analytic judgment of his own and has a thorough knowledge of Aristotle to supply the gap.

The Poetics has been among the most influential of all Aristotle's works. There were ten editions of the text in Italy alone between 1508 and 1572, and between 1543 and the end of the century no fewer than twenty-five printed commentaries. The great Scaliger termed him "perpetual dictator in all the arts" and Ben Jonson, while repudiating the right of any man to that office, allowed him to be "the first accurate critic and truest judge . . . the world ever had." Ironically the most famous theory buttressed by Aristotle's authority cannot be found in his work at all. This is the doctrine of the three unities. Unity of action Aristotle certainly did demand (1451a32). On time he stated as an observed fact that tragedies tend to confine their action to a single circuit of the sun; this observation is turned into a dogma by Cintio, Robortelli, and Segni. The dogma of unity of place is due to Castelvetro. In the Baroque period these views ruled as law, and provided a disciplined framework for Corneille and Racine and a straitjacket for writers of less ability; we may guess that the supposed authority of Aristotle in fact weighed less in the scale than the political mood of the age, the insistence on order and fear of anarchy. The true power of Aristotle's analysis is seen in modern criticism which may owe nothing or little to him directly, but is similar in approach. The work of Brooks Otis in the classical field is one illustration: he is predominantly concerned with structural values. Cleanth Brooks in *The Well-Wrought Urn* shows the same mood. O Aristotle, thou art mighty yet!

CHAPTER 10

Conclusion: The Legacy of Aristotle

WHEN Aristotle withdrew to Chalcis after Alexander's death he left Theophrastus to carry on the University he had founded, and in his will charged Theophrastus with the care of his mistress and children as well as with the property. Theophrastus was a man of genuine intellectual eminence.[1] As they said of the Stoics, "Zeno was the founder, but had there been no Chrysippus there would have been no Stoa," so it is not unjust to say that had there been no Theophrastus there would have been no Peripatos. Theophrastus had a great reputation, and his lecture audience numbered as many as two thousand. He was not an original philosopher, but he had a scholarly and scientific mind; he supplemented Aristotle's zoological work with his own systematic researches into botany; wrote on mineralogy, meteorology, logic, psychology, music, literature, ethics, politics, theology, and much besides, including a major *History of Natural Philosophy*. Of almost equal importance for the Peripatetic School is his friendship with kings. It was a new age of supranational autocracy, and exclusive Athenian nationalism could not prevail. His former pupil, Demetrius of Phalerum, contrary to Athenian practice, allowed him, an alien from Lesbos, to purchase an estate, which he willed to the University community. The University was thus established for the future, and set along the lines of the systematic recording and interpretation of scientific fact, which was always the strength of the Aristotelians. Like any University it had its ups and downs, but it remained, with Platonists, Stoics, and Epicureans, one of the four great institutions of higher education in Athens even into Byzantine times.

Meanwhile, Aristotle's own works suffered curious vicissitudes.[2] On Aristotle's death he left them with Theophrastus. But when Theophrastus died they passed not to Strato, Theophrastus's successor, but to Neleus, who took them with him to Scepsis, where his heirs, being in Strabo's words *idiotai* (we could hardly have a better example on the way the word changes from "private individuals" through "people without a sense of public responsibility" to "idiots"), hid them from the acquisitive tendencies of the reigning dynasty of Pergamum. There they remained concealed for a century and a half till 100 B.C. when they were found and taken to Athens. Shortly after, Sulla acquired them for Rome, and Andronicus and Tyrannio edited and published them, bringing the Aristotelian University into new prominence in the process.

The Romans were interested only in the now lost dialogues and the treatise on *Creative Writing*. Cicero is aware of the dialogues and the treatises, but he quotes only the dialogues, and evidently found the treatises too hard and insufficiently practical. But in Greece from the third to the sixth century there was considerable interest in the treatises, and numerous commentators worked on them; Alexander of Aphrodisias about 200 A.D. stands way above the others in the quality of his interpretation; Simplicius in the sixth century is also important; for the rest we may mention Themistius, Philoponus, Ammonius, Syrianus. In the meantime the great Neoplatonist Porphyry had written a work called *Introduction;* it is in fact an introduction to the logical treatises. This was translated into Latin by Boethius, and Boethius's rendering of Porphyry, together with some of his own comments, was the source of the scholastic knowledge of Aristotle's logic up to the twelfth century.

In the sixth century Justinian closed the pagan universities, and except in the monasteries of Constantinople the Greek world also forgot Aristotle. But versions in Syriac survived and with the dominance of Islam were translated into Arabic and stimulated the creative period of Islamic thought.

The great period of the translators was 750–900. Of the Islamic scholars who seized on them four stand out.[3] Alkindi, who died in 873, took up the idea of the Active Intellect, external to human minds and enlightening them, and made it part of his theological system. In the next century Alfarabi carried the idea further, blending Islam, Aristotle, and Plato. He suggested that the Active Intellect implants the Platonic Forms in our minds. Alfarabi used Aristotelian logic, and it was he who made the logical and metaphysical distinction between existence and essence, the first an accident of the second, thus making possible the distinction between contingent and necessary being, and so the concept of a world causally dependent on God. Alfarabi's view of the end of life for man in the contemplation of God is highly Aristotelian.

More familiar, a man of less original but more comprehensive genius, is Ibn Sina (980–1037); Latin speakers called him Avicenna. A doctor by profession, his restless mind ranged far and wide, and he became the chief interpreter of Aristotle to the medieval world. Rightly, for he reduced the Neo-Platonic accretions encrusting the Aristotle known to Islam. It was Ibn Sina who propounded the doctrine that universals, the Platonic Forms, exist before particular objects in the mind of God, in particular objects in nature, after particular objects in our experience. It was Ibn Sina who similarly distinguished three aspects of essences, being in themselves the appropriate object of metaphysics, in particular things as the object of science, and in our minds as the object of logic. Ibn Sina retained Aristotle's treatment of form and matter as relative terms; at the top of the ladder of being is the divine power, the uncaused cause of the universe, the unmoved mover, who rules of necessity; so Ibn Sina equates Aristotle's Unmoved Mover with the absolute majesty of Allah. It is ironical that Ibn Sina, regarded as dangerously unorthodox by Islam, should have been instrumental in providing Christendom with its orthodoxy.

Finally, Ibn Roshd, or Averröes (1126–98)[4] was one of those scholars who thrive on the interpretation of others. He called Aristotle "a rule and exemplar devised by nature to show the final perfection of man." Aristotle's teaching was the supreme truth, his mind the final expression of the human mind. "Wherefore it has been well said that he was created and given to us by divine providence that we might know all there is to be known. Let us praise God, who set this man apart from all others in perfection, and made him approach very near to the highest dignity humanity can attain." Ibn Roshd's purpose was to present Aristotle to the world pure and undefiled, and his monumental commentary was the result; it won him Dante's approbation. But Aristotle was not the Prophet. Ibn Roshd sought to reconcile them by a doctrine of different levels of truth; for the man in the street the word of revelation, for the man of moderate education probable argument, for the philosopher complete demonstration. It is unjust to Ibn Roshd—not least to his Aristotelianism—to suggest that he held that two incompatible statements might both be true; the necessary conclusion of reason was true, the other the nearest expression of truth that a simple mind could bear. This did not save Ibn Roshd, a patently sincere Muslim, from the charge of unorthodoxy; he ended his life in exile.

Ibn Sina and Ibn Roshd justly had an international reputation. Their commentaries were translated into Hebrew and from Hebrew into Latin, and in the Latin made a tremendous impact in Europe. It is ironic that at first the scholastics were working from a Latin version of a Hebrew version of Arabic commentaries on an Arabic version of a Syriac version of a Greek original. (The story of the spurious work *On Plants* is even odder. Aristotle did write such a work, but it is lost. The work we have is probably owed to an Aristotelian named Nicolaus of Damascus somewhere about the beginning of the Christian era. This work was translated into Arabic by Ishaq Ibn Hunain in the ninth century; from Arabic into Latin by an Englishman, Alfred of Sareshel, in the thirteenth; and incidentally into Hebrew by a Provençal, Qalonymus ben Qalonymus, in the fifteenth; and our Greek text is a retranslation of the Latin).

At first the main interest was in logic; for cosmology the Church tried to blend Aristotle with Plato's *Timaeus;* in metaphysics they were divided between realists like the doctors of Chartres (a realist in mediaeval thought being one who believes in the reality of the Platonic Form, not of the material world) holding that "universals are real entities existing before the material thing," and nominalists like Roscelin or Ockham, holding that "universals are mere names and exist after the material object," with in between moderate realists like Abelard, holding that "universals are real entities immanent in the material object," [5] a position which approximately represents the view of Aristotle. It is astonishing that the main controversy—though it was left to Ockham to clinch the matter—was worked out before the rediscovery of Aristotle.

Logic—and the problem of universals—was followed by concentration on the nature of the soul and its faculties. Ibn Sina and Ibn Roshd had both treated of this, and Ibn Sina's interpretation was taken up in the middle of the twelfth century by an Italian cleric named Dominic Gundisalvi: the soul is both form and substance and is made by God out of spiritual matter. Its passive or potential Intellect needs to be actualized by Active Intellect, namely God.

Already, in the twelfth century James of Venice had visited Constantinople and found the Greek manuscripts; he translated the logic, which was avidly seized on, and the psychology and metaphysics which proved tougher fare. Then in 1204 Christian Constantinople was sacked by the Crusaders, and this otherwise disastrous episode helped to renew the contact. Latin versions of the Greek, not dependent on Arabic intermediaries, gradually began to penetrate the consciousness of the West. It was the authentic Aristotle who molded the thought of the great doctors of the thirteenth century, Albertus Magnus and Thomas Aquinas. It is needful to remember that Aristotle did not appear as a conservative force but as a dangerous revolutionary. In 1210 the provincial synod of Sens decreed, "Neither the writings of Aristotle on natural philosophy nor their commentaries are to be read," i.e., taught "at Paris in public or private, and this we forbid under penalty of excommunication."[6] It is amusing that other authors banned under the same decree include Maurice of Spain; no such person is known and it is probably a mistake for "the Spanish Moor," i.e. Ibn Roshd.

Five years later, Cardinal Robert de Curzon, laying down statutes for the University of Paris, forbade lectures "on the books of Aristotle on metaphysics and natural philosophy or on summaries of them; nor concerning the doctrine of master David of Dinant" (a somewhat erratic interpreter of Aristotle) "and the heretic Anaury of Spain." This was reinforced by papal decree. As well might Mrs. Partington attempt to hold back the Atlantic Ocean with her mop. In the 1230s Aristotle's *Ethics* was one of the textbooks. At Oxford there was no ban, and Roger Bacon came to Paris to lecture on Aristotle's *Physics* and *Metaphysics.* By 1252 the psychology was prescribed for English students in Paris; three years later the whole corpus was open to the whole academic body. By now Aristotle was "*the* philosopher" as Paul was "*the* apostle," and further papal proclamation could not stay his authority.

The Franciscans were suspicious of Aristotle. So at first were the Dominicans. It was Albertus Magnus who turned the scale. Unfortunately, the chronology of his voluminous writings is uncertain; one reasonable interpretation divides the work into four periods, the first theological (1228–48), the second concentrating on Aristotle's *Ethics* and the neo-Platonic mysticism of "Dionysius the Areopagite" (1248–54), the third involved with the full exposition of Aristotelianism (1254–70), the fourth again theological (1270–80). Albertus was aiming at a comprehensive critical commentary. He is not a blinkered Aristotelian; he values Plato alongside Aristotle (though in his doctrine of universals he sides with Aristotle), and he knows that neither offers a pure Christian view.

Albertus would loom larger if he were not overshadowed by the mighty figure of Thomas Aquinas. For Aquinas was one of the dominant intellectual figures of all history; alongside his powerful synthesis we cannot help seeing Albertus, for all his learning, as inconsistent in his own thinking and miscellaneous in his criticism. Aquinas's genius lay in the fact that he was able to comprehend in a single philosophical system, which we rightly call Thomism, for it was new and unique, his Christian faith, a thoroughgoing Aristotelianism and a blending in of important elements of Platonism. This he did first by marking off the sphere of reason from the sphere of revelation, so that he was able to dismiss Aristotle from the second. But he did not regard the findings of reason as in any way contrary to those of revelation. There is only one truth, but there are aspects of it which reason unaided cannot reach. Reason is wholly adequate to attain truth within the sensible world and to reach out from its experience of the sensible world to God as the prime cause. Grace does not destroy nature; it perfects it. His metaphysics and epistemology are taken over lock, stock, and barrel from Aristotle, and treated with clarity and subtlety—necessary and contingent being, actuality and potentiality, form and matter, are all set to the service of the Christian God.

Thomas died in 1274. Meanwhile at Paris the brilliant but erratic Siger of Brabant was stirring up opposition to an Aristotelianism of his own, and in 1277 Bishop Tempier issued a comprehensive but hasty condemnation of some 219 propositions of the Aristotelians. Thomas was not mentioned by name, but his views came under the censure. The effect was paradoxical. It provoked his friends to a counterattack. Tempier's condemnation was rescinded, and Thomas was canonized. The conservatives might not like it, but large segments of Aristotle had crept into Christian orthodoxy. The revolutionary was in fact swallowed by the establishment. There is a sense in which it was in the name of Aristotle that Bruno was burnt at the stake and Galileo forced to recant.

The Renaissance saw an impetus to Aristotelian studies through the invention of printing; this was the age of Zabarella, one of the greatest of Aristotelian commentators. At the same time it was a period of reaction. This was partly a natural swing of the pendulum after a period of excessive concentration, so to speak an Aristotelian reaction against Aristotelianism. (So did Karl Barth say "Thank God I am not a Barthian.") It was partly a reaction against the dogmatic authority of the church, which had made of Aristotle an infallible authority. Voltaire was to say, "We hiss them off the stage then, those rude scholastics who have tyrannized over us for so long. We honor [rather unexpectedly] Cicero, who taught us how to think." It was partly a commonsense reaction against scholasticism. Bacon, Galileo, and Boyle all spoke of his authority with bitter scorn, and Thomas Hobbes wrote in *Leviathan:* "I believe that scarce anything can be more absurdly said in natural philosophy, than that which now is called Aristotle's *Metaphysics;* nor more repugnant to government, than much of that he hath said in his *Politics;* nor more ignorantly, than a great part of his *Ethics.*" [7] It was still more a literary reaction. Petrarch already had had no time for Aristotle. The treatises are singularly lacking in literary graces; in the seventeenth and eighteenth centuries they were read by philosophers like Locke and Berkeley, but by few others. Only *Poetics* remained, and it, as we have seen, was used to impose a classicism that Aristotle did not hold.

Modern Aristotelian studies begin effectively with the publication of the great Berlin edition of 1831. The first two volumes contain the text edited by Bekker with the fragmentary remains added by Rose, the third volume has the Latin versions, the fourth has the scholia or ancient annotations, and the fifth was an invaluable index compiled by Bonitz. But the nineteenth century tended to treat Aristotle as the expounder of a single monolithic system, and though solid work was achieved earlier, two twentieth century scholars have done most to reveal the true Aristotle. Werner Jaeger, whatever controversy there may be about the details of his scheme, revealed a dynamic, developing philosophy, alive and vital. Sir David Ross produced a succession of editions and commentaries notable alike for their monumental learning, their sympathetic understanding, and the soundness of their judgment. Alongside this, papers on detailed aspects of Aristotle's works pour out in learned journals all over the world, and there is no slackening of the spate. At the same time he was brought nearer the intelligent non-specialist. The decade 1958–68 saw at least three new volumes of translated selections available to the American public in addition to those already circulating, and (to take one work alone) at least six new expositions of *Poetics*.

Why, we may ask, does Aristotle survive? Why are we still concerned with him?

First, he is among the great rationalists. He believes that the universe is a rational order and that human reason is competent to comprehend it. This insistence on reason has been the driving power of all scientific investigation. The horizons of the universe have receded vastly since Aristotle's day, but that does not make scientists less eager to probe them, or less certain that if we devise the right tools we can probe them. Aristotle's universe was geocentric. Copernican theory has been displaced by Relativity, and the universe of the modern scientist remains irreducibly anthropocentric. The philosophers of science may deny the possibility of certainty, but the practising scientist aspires towards it. The epigram about the physicist who holds a wave-theory of light on Monday, Wednesday, and Friday, a corpuscular theory on Tuesday, Thursday, and Saturday—and on Sunday prays to his own particular gods that he may be the one to reconcile them—is completed by its final clause. Confidence in reason is the nuclear power by which science soars into space.

Second, Aristotle is a pioneer of scientific method. Scientific method was succinctly summarized by Francis Bacon: observe, measure, explain, verify. With advancing techniques this was refined to: pose a question about nature, collect pertinent evidence, form an explanatory hypothesis, deduce its implications, test them experimentally, and then accept, reject, or modify the hypothesis accordingly. The first four of these represent Aristotle's methodology, as by and large they remain the methodology of the field naturalist; only the experimental techniques of the laboratory did he lack. What is more, it represents the technique of all scholarship, of history, or literary criticism, for instance. This methodology he bequeathed to the Lyceum, and through them to the great Alexandrian scientists. Would you study zoology or botany? Collect specimens. Would you study politics? Collect constitutions and the history of their workability. Would you study ethics? Collect "characters." Would you study creative writing? Collect plays, and audience-reaction to them. Would you study logic? Collect fallacies. And where this method is less obviously applicable, at least collect and sift the opinions of your predecessors, as Aristotle does in the first book of *Metaphysics* and at the beginning of *Physics, Psychology,* and *On Coming-to-be and Passing-away* as well as at significant points elsewhere. Pose a question, collect pertinent evidence, form an explanatory hypothesis, deduce its implications. It is a good account of Aristotle's procedure. "Je m'attache pour l'ordre" says a character in Molière's *Les Femmes Savantes* "au péripatétisme." Indeed.

Third, Aristotle is impressive by the very comprehensive nature of his purview. He invented logic, and his use of letters in logic pointed the way, centuries later, to symbolic logic. As a biologist he stands supreme; we have noted Darwin's tribute. His treatise on ethics remains, in a very different society, one of the seminal works; the related work on politics is unfashionable, because "undemocratic," though Aristotle would reflect any modern constitution to be far more undemocratic than anything he advocated, and there is much challenging good sense in the treatise. As a literary critic he seems slighter, but his influence has been immense and that at a time when his general philosophy was widely rejected. Finally, the comprehensive world view found throughout the works, especially in *Physics* and *Metaphysics,* is unfashionable in an age when metaphysics is suspect. It remains one of the great syntheses, and the doctrines of actuality and potentiality, of form and matter, of necessity and accident, are applied with extraordinary subtlety and perspicacity. Roger Bacon paid him a notable tribute when he wrote "Although Aristotle did not arrive at the end of knowledge, he set in order all parts of philosophy."

Fourth, as Marjorie Grene has stressed, Aristotle teaches us to look at the universe biologically. A mechanistic world is a dreary world. A mathematical world is an abstract world. A biological world is a living world, an exciting world, a beautiful world, a world in which vitalism is shared by the comprehending mind and the organisms it comprehends, a world of patterns. How Aristotle would have gloried in the photographs available in modern books of natural history. We might learn this lesson from Bergson or Whitehead—and we do well not to forget them. But it is Aristotle who teaches it supremely.

Fifth, Aristotle is unashamedly teleological. To most contemporary interpreters this will seem a weakness, unscientific. But is it? Socrates rejected the question "how?" in favor of the question "why?" Aristotle does no such thing; he asserts that for a full explanation the question "why?" must come in alongside the question "how?" That it is in certain circumstances a relevant question is clear; the famous account of violin playing in material terms as rubbing the entrails of a dead sheep with the hairs of a dead horse is, as A. D. Ritchie once said, trivial unless the performance is very bad; it is inadequate, incomplete; it requires an object, an aim, a *telos*. An account of the movement of billiard balls in terms of the material composition of cue, cloth, cushions and balls, the force imparted by the striker's arm, and the subsequent pattern of movement, is incomplete without the teleology which the rules of the game might supply.

But in the field of biology it might seem that Darwin had thrown teleology out of the window for once and for all. In fact the amount of almost wistful, half-conscious teleological language used by modern biologists is remarkable. I open a recent book, and find on almost every page something like: "Why does an animal behave the way it does?"; "There was a reason for the gulls' habit of all laying their eggs at about the same time."; "The quest for the causes underlying behavior"; "Von Frisch wanted to know *why* the fish came when he whistled"; "Contorted in defense, a larva of a noctuid moth raises itself to scare off a predator." [8] What is in question is not of course a theory of evolution; Aristotle was wrong in holding fixity of species. It is whether there is room for teleology in evolutionary theory. There remain examples not easily to be explained in terms of chance variation. Asa Gray, followed by Bergson, instanced the eye; J. A. Lowell, and, with far vaster evidence, Fabre cited the incredibly complex instinctual behavior of insects; others have taken the parasitism of the cuckoo, the life-cycle of the liverfluke (subject of a notable parable in James Bridie's *Mr. Bolfry*), or Sir Charles Sherrington's account of the malaria plasmodium (Sherrington's own interpretation is halting and uneasy).[9] Certainly the wholesale rejection of natural teleology should be recognized for what it is, a piece of dogmatic assertiveness which has no place in science.

But apart from biology there are certain fields, notably aesthetics and ethics, where it is at the least not obvious that language is being used descriptively. We are dealing with values, norms, ends. The question "why?" does not permit such a straightforward answer as the question "how?" Excessive concentration upon it might lead to idle speculation instead of solid research; a false assurance of having answered it in the only way possible might lead to a dogmatism which stood in the path of new knowledge. This was a trap Aristotle never fell into. He was too good a scientist, too solid a believer in "thisness." Fact came before interpretation. But for our ultimate understanding of life, the "why?" is ineluctable.

This leads to the last point. In some ways the most impressive feature of Aristotle is not the grandeur of his system, but his solid detailed commonsense. It shines even from his lecture-illustrations. Henry Jackson was able to reconstruct Aristotle's lecture-room from the illustrations in his lectures;[10] Aristotle had an earthy awareness of his environment. It shines from his rejection of fantasy and "way-out" theories, even though they come from Plato; there is a cutting decisiveness about "Man may be a formula expressible numerically, but he is not a number." It is the basis of his ethics and politics.

Aristotle has been accused of authoritarianism.[11] Almost the reverse is true. He has such respect for the opinions of the average man that he rationalizes them even when they are irrational. This explains parts of his philosophy which we find repugnant, as his defense of slavery. Only a few cranks and visionaries challenged slavery. Aristotle was no saint; he stuck to the middle of the road. It is at once a weakness and strength in ethics and politics; it makes him a reformer not a revolutionary. But in his general world-picture it is a great strength. For he is free from otherworldliness. His thought is rooted in particularity, in *this.*

Werner Jaeger called him "the founder of scientific philosophy"; Dante, "the master of those that know."

Notes and References

Chapter Two

1. Cic. *Acad.* 2, 38, 119; Quint. 10, 1, 83.
2. *Protrepticus:* important attempts at reconstruction by I. Düring (Gothoburg, 1961) and A.-H. Chroust (Notre Dame, 1964).
3. Jaeger: p. 155.
4. *The Theology of Aristotle:* see the appendix to the Henry-Schwyzer edition of Plotinus's *Enneads,* vol. 2.

Chapter Three

1. The most useful work is J. L. Ackrill, *Aristotle's Categories and De Intepretatione* (Oxford, 1963). For other important discussions see E. Kapp, *The Greek Foundations of Traditional Logic* (New York 1942) 36–42; J. Owens in *Review of Metaphysics* 14 (1960) 73–90; G. Ryle in A. Flew, *Logic and Language* (New York, 1965) 281–98.
2. Socratic schools: see O. Apelt, *Beiträge zur Geschichte der Griechischen Philosophie.*
3. Substance: see the important paper by J. P. Anton in *Monist* 52 (1968) 252 ff in opposition to J. Owens, *The Doctrine of Being in the Aristotelian Metaphysics* (Toronto, 1951); also "Aristotle on Categories" *Rev. of Metaph.* 14 (1960) 73–90.
4. John Locke: *An Essay Concerning Human Understanding* bk. iv c. 5, cited by H. P. Cooke in his introduction to the Loeb *Categories.*
5. I owe this presentation to Prof. D. M. Balme.
6. P. F. Strawson. *Introduction to Logical Theory* (New York, 1952) p. 1.
7. For the date see W. D. Ross, ed., *Prior and Posterior Analytics* (Oxford, 1949), an indispensable work, against F. Solmsen, *Die Entwicklung der aristotelischen Logik und Rhetorik* (Berlin, 1929). For the fundamental principles see H. D. P. Lee in *CQ* 29 (1935), 113–29.
8. Ross, *Aristotle* p. 51.
9. Plato, *Phaedr.* 265d; 277b; *Soph* 218d.
10. Tredennick in his introduction to the Loeb *Post. An.* p. 17.
11. G. E. M. Anscombe and P. Geach, *Three Philosophers* (Ithaca, 1961) p. 6.
12. *Topics:* for the date see H. Maier, *Die Syllogistik des Aristoteles*

(Tübingen 1900); F. Solmsen *op. cit.;* P. Gohlke *Die Entstehung der aristotelischen Logik* (Berlin, 1936).

13. Ross, *Aristotle,* p. 59; Jonson, *The Silent Woman,* II 3 (I owe this reference to Dr. Ruth Mohl).

14. "Still warm remembrance" from *The Solace of Leisure Hours; or Essays of Poesy* by A. Sailor (Robert Peters), (London, 1875). The next line is "Thee, M. M. Woods, forget I'll never!"

15. B. Russell, *History of Western Philosophy* (London 1946) p. 225. Contrast A. N. Whitehead in *Proc. Ar. Soc.* N.S. 17, p. 72; L. S. Stebbing, *A Modern Introduction to Logic* (London 1933), p. 164.

Chapter Four

1. The contraries: J. Ferguson, "The Opposites," *Apeiron* 3 (1969) 1–17.

2. Privation: *Met.* V 1022b22; IX 1046a32; X 1055a34; XII 1070b-11 etc.

3. S. Bochner, *The Role of Mathematics in the Rise of Science* (Princeton, 1966).

4. Bochner, *op. cit.*

5. Ross, *Aristotle's Physics* p. 71. Zeno: the literature on the paradoxes is immense. See Cajori, F., "The History of Zeno's arguments on Motion" in *Am. Math. Monthly* 22 (1915); Lee, H. D. P. *Zeno of Elea* (Cambridge, 1936).

6. Seventh book: see conveniently Ross's introduction.

7. *On the Universe:* the best guide is W. K. C. Guthrie's Loeb edition; J. L. Stocks's version in the Oxford translation has useful notes.

8. Ross, *Aristotle* p. 95.

9. Mars: Guthrie *ad loc.,* quoting K. Schloch, *Planetentafeln für Jedermann* (Berlin, 1927) col. XX.

10. "changing informations": from H. H. Joachim *ad loc.*

11. Descartes, *Princ. Phil.,* part 4, par. 204.

12. Circumference of the earth: *C.* 2,298a10.

13. Winds: D'Arcy Thompson, "The Greek Winds" *CR* 32 (1918) 49–56.

14. Book IV: I. Düring, *Aristotle's Chemical Treatise Meteorologica Book IV* (Göteborg, 1944), as against I. Hammer-Jensen, "Das sogennante IV. Buch der Meteorologie des Aristoteles" *Herm.* (1915) 113–36.

15. G. H. Lewes, *Aristotle* (London, 1864), pp. 67–8.

Chapter Five

1. G. Cuvier, *Histoire des Sciences Naturelles* (Paris, 1841) I, p. 146.

2. H. D. P. Lee, "Placenames and the Date of Aristotle's Biological Works" *CQ* 42 (1948) 61 ff.

3. A. Steier, *Aristoteles und Plinius*, p. 113.

4. C. R. Burckhardt, "Das erste Buch der aristotelischen Tiergeschichte," *Zoolog. Ann.* 1 (1905) 1–28.

5. Sea anemone: *P.A.* 681*b*1.

6. G. H. Lewes, *Aristotle* (London, 1864), p. 285.

7. cuttlefish: D. W. Thompson, *Science and the Classics* (Oxford, 1940), 49 ff.

8. *Mustelus laevis:* the smooth dog fish: see Müller, J. "Uber d. glatten Hus des Aristoteles (*Mustelus laevis*)" *Abh.d.Berl.Akad.*, 1846.

9. cicadas: Plin. *NH* 11, 32; see also Ael. *VH* 5, 9; Antig. *Mirab.* 3.

10. H. Bergson, *L'Évolution Créatrice*, c.i.

11. Fabre: see *The Hunting Wasps.*

12. jumping: see Gardiner, E. N., *Athletics of the Ancient World* (Oxford 1930) p. 151.

13. Boyle, *Of the Usefulnesse of Naturall Philosophy*, cited by A. L. Peck in the Loeb edition.

14. Bacon: See *Advancement of Learning*, Book II.

15. Darwin: Darwin F. *The Life and Letters of Charles Darwin* (London 1887) III 252.

16. Mrs. Harris: Dickens, *Martin Chuzzlewit*, c. 46, cited by Platt in the Oxford translation *ad loc.*

17. Lewes, p. 382.

Chapter Six

1. R. D. Hicks, *Aristotle: De Anima* (Cambridge, 1907) has not been completely outmoded by Ross as an annotated edition of the Greek text.

2. On "common sensibility": W. D. Ross, *Aristotle*, pp. 140 ff is challengingly criticized by D. W. Hamlyn in *The Monist*, 52 (1968), 195 ff. On the relative dates of *De Anima, Parva Naturalia* see Block, I. "The order of Aristotle's psychological writings" *AJP*, 82 (1961) 50 ff. against W. D. Ross, *Parva Naturalia* (Oxford, 1955); F. Nuyens, *L'évolution de la psychologie d'Aristote* (Louvain, 1948).

3. On the intellect thinking itself: R. Norman, "Aristotle's Philosopher-God" *Phronesis* 14 (1969) 63 ff.

4. On active and passive reason there is a sensible article by J. M. Rist *C.Ph.* 61 (1966) 8 ff.

5. *Parva Naturalia:* Ross's edition is standard in English, but there is also an acute commentary on the treatise on sleep and dreams by H. J. D. Lulofs *De Sommo et Vigilia* (Templum Salomonis, 1943); *De Insomniis et De Divinatione per Somnum*, 2 vols. (Leyden, 1947).

6. Plato: *Theaetetus*, 191c8 ff.

7. Plato: *Phaed.* 73d2 ff.

8. Ross, pp. 40.3.

9. It is almost unbelievable that as late as 1935 the Loeb translator felt that this innocent passage must be rendered into Latin not English.

10. J. W. Dunne, *An Experiment with Time* (London 1927); J. B. Priestley: esp. *Time and the Conways* (London 1937).

11. J. Ferguson, "The Opposites," *Apeiron* 3 (1969), 1–17.

Chapter Seven

1. W. Jaeger, *Aristoteles* (Berlin, 1923).

2. H. Cherniss, *Aristotle's Criticism of Pre-Socratic Philosophy* (Baltimore, 1935), p. 404.

3. Plato *Phaedo* 100d.

4. Plato *Soph.* 254e.

5. W. D. Ross, ed., *Aristotle's Metaphysics,* 2 vols. (Oxford, 1924), (the fundamental commentary) lxxvii.

6. Privation: The main passages are *Met.* V 1022b22; IX 1046a32; X 1055a34; XII 1070b11; *Phys.* II 193b20; but there are many others.

7. Plato *Rep.* VI 507d; *Theaet.* 197a ff.

8. "coping-stone": Ross, *Aristotle,* p. 179.

9. Mind thinks itself; see R. Norman, "Aristotle's Philosopher-God," *Phronesis* 14 (1969) 63 ff.

10. The whole matter is highly controversial. For a thorough discussion see T. L. Heath, *Aristarchus of Samos* (Oxford 1913), pp. 190–224.

11. Hom. *Il.* 2, 204.

Chapter Eight

1. *Magna Moralia:* H. von Arnim, F. Dirlmeier and I. Düring claim it as authentic Aristotle.

2. Henry Jackson: R. St. J. Parry, *Henry Jackson, O.M.* (Cambridge, 1926), p. 158.

3. Happiness: see the papers of H. A. Prichard and J. L. Austin in J. M. E. Moravcsik *Aristotle* (New York, 1967), pp. 241–96.

4. J. Fletcher, *Situation Ethics.*

5. *Megalopsychia:* see Dorothea Kroot *Three Traditions of Moral Thought* (Cambridge, 1959).

6. R. Bambrough: *New Essays on Plato and Aristotle* (London, 1965), pp. 159 ff.

7. P. Huby: *Greek Ethics* (New York, 1967), p. 44.

8. J. Burnet: *The Ethics of Aristotle* (London, 1900), *ad loc.*

9. Practical good sense: see P. Aubenque, *La Prudence chez Aristote* (Paris, 1963).

10. Incontinence: see J. J. Walsh *Aristotle's Conception of Moral Weakness* (New York 1963); R. Robinson, "L'acrasie selon Aristote"

Rév. Phil. 145 (1955) 261–80; G. E. M. Anscombe *Intention* (Oxford 1957) pp. 57 ff.

11. Ovid: *Met.* 7, 20.
12. Paul: *Rom.* 7, 19.
13. Practical syllogism: see D. J. Allan "The Practical Syllogism" in *Autour d'Aristote* (Louvain 1955).
14. Pleasure: see J. O. Urmson, "Aristotle on Pleasure" in J. M. E. Moravcsik, *op. cit.* 323–33; A.-J. Festugière *Aristote, Le Plaisir* (Paris 1936); G. Liebig *Die Lehre von der Lust in den Ethiken des Aristoteles* (München 1958).
15. Plato: *Phileb.* 60 ff.
16. J. Burnet: *op. cit.* pp. 344–45.
17. P. B. Shelley: *A Defence of Poetry.*
18. One scholar: J. Léonard *Le Bonheur chez Aristote* (Brussels 1948).
19. The whole matter is highly controversial. One of the controversial views is in W. Jaeger, *Aristotle* (E. T. Oxford, 1948^{2}); another H. von Arnim *Zur Entstehungsgeschichte der aristotelischen Politik.* See also J. L. Stocks in *CQ* 21 (1927), 177–87; E. Barker in *CR* 45 (1931), 162–72.
20. Lycurgus: E. Barker, *The Politics of Aristotle* (Oxford, 1952), xxi.
21. Montesquieu: see E. Barker, *The Political Thought of Plato and Aristotle* (London, 1906), p. 484.
22. J. Donne: *Devotions upon Emergent Occasions,* XVII.
23. R. Bambrough: *The Philosophy of Aristotle* (New York 1963) p. 381. Some phrases in this chapter are repeated from my *Moral Values in the Ancient World* (London, 1958).

Chapter Nine

1. L. Cooper, *The Rhetoric of Aristotle* (New York, 1932) p. xvii.
2. W. D. Ross, *Aristotle,* p. 275.
3. E. Copleston, *A Reply to the Calumnies of the Edinburgh Review against Oxford,* pp. 26–7, cited by Cooper p. xi.
4. 1420b4, cf. Lys. *In Erat,* ad fin.
5. F. L. Lucas, *Tragedy,* p. 92.
6. Comedy: L. Cooper, *An Aristotelian Theory of Comedy* (Ithaca, 1922). Not all accept Lane Cooper's views.

Chapter Ten

1. Theophrastus: Diog. Laert. 4, 36–57; O. Regenbogen in *PW* suppl. vol. vii s.v. Theophrastos.
2. Transmission of Aristotle: R. Shute, *On the History of the Process by which the Aristotelian Writings arrived at their present form* (Ox-

ford, 1888); J. E. Sandys: *A History of Classical Scholarship* (Cambridge ^{2}1920). The cardinal texts are Strabo 13, 608; Plutarch *Sulla* 26, 1–2.

3. See J. Ferguson, "The Influence of Greek Philosophy on Islam" in L. A. Thompson and J. Ferguson (ed.). *Classical Influences in Africa* (Ibadan U.P., Nigeria, 1969).

4. Ibn Roshd: B. Geyer: *Die patrische und scholastische Philosophie* (Berlin, 1938), p. 316: Dante *Inferno* 4, 144.

5. The epigram comes from E. Renan, *Averroès et l'Averroisme* (Paris ^{2}1861), p. 52.

6. Paris: H. Denifle and A. Chatelain *Chartularium Universitatis Parisiensis* (Paris 1889–97).

7. Hobbes, *Leviathan IV*, 46.

8. The quotations are from N. Tinbergen, *Animal Behavior* (New York, 1965).

9. C. Sherrington: *Man on his Nature* (Cambridge ^{2}1951) pp. 369–75 cf. 187. In general see C. E. Raven, *Science, Religion and the Future* (Cambridge, 1943) for a remarkable brief conspectus.

10. H. Jackson: "Aristotle's Lecture-Room and Lectures" *J. Ph.* 35 (1920) pp. 191 ff.

11. Authoritarianism: as by G. E. R. Lloyd *Aristotle: The Growth and Structure of his Thought* (Cambridge, 1968), p. 305.

For Further Reading

It is better to read an author than to read about him. Aristotle's complete works are available in English:

Ross, W. D. (ed.). *The Works of Aristotle.* 12 vols. Oxford, 1928–52.

A convenient short selection, paperbound, with new translations, is:

Bambrough, J. R. (ed.). *The Philosophy of Aristotle.* (Mentor Books MY 804), New York, 1963.

Unfortunately this selection ignores the biological works. This is remedied in a fuller hardbound selection:

McKeon, R. (ed.). *The Basic Works of Aristotle.* New York, 1941.

The Loeb Classical Library has now published virtually the whole of Aristotle. These volumes give the Greek texts with facing translation, and for Aristotle notes of considerable helpfulness. The series as a whole is of uneven value, but the Aristotle volumes are mostly of a high quality. Individual works are conveniently available in English:

Aristotle. *On Poetry and Style,* tr. G. M. A. Grube. (Library of Liberal Arts 68), New York, 1958.

Hope, R. (tr.) *Aristotle's Physics* (Bison Books 122). Lincoln, 1961.

Sinclair, T. A. (tr.) *The Politics of Aristotle.* (Penguin), Baltimore, 1962.

Warrington, J. (tr.) *Aristotle's Metaphysics* (Everyman), London, 1956.

The following are the more useful editions for English-speaking readers of the Greek text with full annotations:

Metaphysics, ed. W. D. Ross. 2 vols. Oxford, 1924.

Physics, ed. W. D. Ross. Oxford, 1936.

Prior and Posterior Analytics, ed. W. D. Ross. Oxford, 1949.

Parva Naturalia, ed. W. D. Ross. Oxford, 1955.

De Anima, ed. W. D. Ross. Oxford, 1961.

De Anima, ed. R. D. Hicks. Cambridge, 1907.

Ethics, ed. J. Burnet. London, 1900.

Politics, ed. W. L. Newman. 4 vols. Oxford, 1887–1902.

Politics I–V, ed. F. Susemihl and R. D. Hicks. London, 1894.

On Coming-to-be and Passing-away, ed. H. H. Joachim. Oxford, 1922.
Poetics, ed. D. W. Lucas. Oxford, 1968.
Poetics, ed. G. F. Else. Cambridge, Mass., 1957.
Rhetoric, ed. E. M. Cope and J. E. Sandys. 3 vols. Cambridge, 1877.

The following have notes on the Greek text without the actual text:

Joachim, H. H. *Aristotle: the Nicomachean Ethics*. Oxford, 1950.
Stewart, J. A. *Notes on the Nicomachean Ethics*. Oxford, 1892.

The following are the more useful editions for English-speaking readers of an English translation with annotations:

Categories and De Interpretatione, ed. J. L. Ackrill. Oxford, 1963.
De Anima Books II and III (with certain passages from Book I), ed. D. W. Hamlyn. Oxford, 1968.
De Partibus Animalium I et De Generatione Animalium I trs. D. M. Balme.
Physics Books I and II ed. W. Charlton. Oxford 1970.
Politics, ed. E. Barker. Oxford, 1952.
Politics Books III and IV, ed. R. Robinson. Oxford, 1962.
Poetics, ed. L. Golden and O. B. Hardison. Englewood Cliffs, 1968.

The Oxford translation (see above) is especially useful on the biological works, which are well annotated.

It is useful to see Aristotle's thought, both in its totality and in its different aspects, against the general background of Greek thought. The best single-volume history of Greek philosophy is:

Copleston, F. C. *A History of Philosophy*. Vol. I. New York, [2]1962.

Other aspects of his work are placed in context in:

Kneale, W. and M. *The Development of Logic*. Oxford, 1962.
Singer, C. *Greek Biology and Greek Medicine*. Oxford, 1922.
Sinclair, T. A. *A History of Greek Political Thought*. London, 1959.
Sambursky, S. *The Physical World of the Greeks*. London, 1956.
Needham, J. *A History of Embryology*. Cambridge, 1934.

There are a number of good general accounts of Aristotle's thought available in English. The best, a masterpiece of clear, brief exposition, is:

Allan, D. J. *The Philosophy of Aristotle*. Oxford, 1952.

Another clear and attractive book is:

Grene, Marjorie. *A Portrait of Aristotle*. London, 1963.

Brief but stimulating is:

Farrington, B. *Aristotle*. (Pathfinder Biography). London, 1965.

There are two rather heavier books of major importance. The first is the standard work of reference for all matters concerning Aristotle:

Ross, W. D. *Aristotle*. (Meridian 1965), New York, [5]1953.

The other is the most original contribution to Aristotelian studies during this century, a pioneer study of Aristotle's thought as developing instead of static:

Jaeger, W. *Aristotle: Fundamentals of the History of his Development,* tr. R. Robinson. Oxford, ^{2}1948.

Four other conveniently accessible general books should be mentioned; all have merit:

Stocks, J. L. *Aristotelianism.* New York, 1963.
Mure, G. R. G. *Aristotle.* London, 1932.
Randall, J. H., Jr. *Aristotle.* New York, 1960.
Lloyd, G. E. R. *Aristotle: The Growth and Structure of his Thought.* (Paperback CAM 456), Cambridge, 1968.

For a treatment by a very competent contemporary philosopher see:

Anscombe, G. E. M. and Geach, P. *Three Philosophers.* Ithaca, 1961.

On particular aspects consult:

Hardie, W. F. R. *Aristotle's Ethical Theory.* Oxford, 1968.
Barker, E. *The Political Thought of Plato and Aristotle.* London, 1906.
Lones, T. E. *Aristotle's Researches in Natural Science.* London, 1912.
Solmsen, F. *Aristotle's System of the Physical World.* Cornell, 1960.
Owens, J. *The Doctrine of Being in Aristotle's Metaphysics.* Toronto, 1957.[2]

Aristotle's thought was immensely influential later. An excellent book on this is:

Pieper, J. *Scholasticism: Personalities and Problems of Mediaeval Philosophy.* London, 1961.

Those who wish to plunge more deeply into Aristotle's thought should consult the bibliography in:

Düring, I. *Aristoteles: Darstellung und Interpretation seines Denkes.* Heidelberg, 1966.

An almost indispensable tool for further research is:

Bonitz, H. *Index Aristoticus.* Berlin, 1870.

Greekless readers will find a convenient substitute in:

Organ, T. W. *Index to Aristotle in English Translation.* Princeton, 1949.

Index